THE POLITICS OF SECOND GENERATION DISCRIMINATION IN AMERICAN INDIAN EDUCATION

THE POLITICS OF SECOND GENERATION DISCRIMINATION IN AMERICAN INDIAN EDUCATION

Incidence, Explanation, and Mitigating Strategies

David E. Wright, III
Michael W. Hirlinger
Robert E. England

BERGIN & GARVEY
Westport, Connecticut • London

Library of Congress Cataloging-in-Publication Data

Wright, David E., III.
 The politics of second generation discrimination in American
Indian education : incidence, explanation, and mitigating strategies
/ David E. Wright, III, Michael W. Hirlinger, Robert E. England.
  p. cm.
 Includes bibliographical references (p.) and index.
 ISBN 0–89789–531–2 (alk. paper)
 1. Indians of North America—Education. 2. Discrimination in
education—United States. 3. Educational equalization—United
States. 4. Education and state—United States. I. Hirlinger,
Michael W. II. England, Robert E. III. Title.
E97W96 1998
370′.8997—dc21   97–16131

British Library Cataloguing in Publication Data is available.

Library of Congress Catalog Card Number: 97–16131
ISBN: 0–89789–531–2

First published in 1998

Bergin & Garvey, 88 Post Road West, Westport, CT 06881
An imprint of Greenwood Publishing Group, Inc.

Printed in the United States of America

The paper used in this book complies with the
Permanent Paper Standard issued by the National
Information Standards Organization (Z39.48–1984).

10 9 8 7 6 5 4 3 2 1

To Lisa my wife and Logan my son — D.E.W.

To Skyler my daughter and Taylor my son — M. W. H.

To Dian my spouse, Eric and Tony my sons, Buckwheat my dog, and Mantra my cat — R.E.E.

Contents

Tables and Figures

FIGURES

Preface

This book is the results of many influences. We must acknowledge the second generation discrimination research of Meier, Stewart, and England (1989) focusing on African American students and Meier and Stewart (1991) focusing on Hispanic students. This seminal research provides a theoretical and analytical trail others can easily follow. A version of this book first appeared as David Wright's doctoral dissertation, Department of Political Science, University of Houston. David wishes to thank his dissertation chair, Dr. Robert Lineberry, and remaining members of his dissertation committee, Drs. Richard Matland, Greg Weiher, and Robert England.

The Spencer Foundation, Chicago, Illinois, provided a generous grant that allowed us to conduct our case studies. Without the grant, the case studies would not have been possible. The data presented, the statements made, and the views expressed are solely the responsibilities of the authors.

Dean Smith Holt, College of Arts and Sciences, Oklahoma State University, provided us summer research money to prepare the larger grant funded by the Spencer Foundation. Thanks, Smith, for your help and confidence in us. Dr. Toni Shaklee, Arts and Sciences Research, identified the Spencer Foundation to us as a potential funding source; thanks, Toni. Ms. Patricia Pettway helped us navigate the financial waters associated with our grant.

Dr. Linda Warner, University of Missouri and National Science Foundation, provided us an excellent review of the book. Her comments were most helpful, and the research effort benefited greatly from her advice and encouragement. As an American Indian of the Comanche tribe, an educational policy expert, and widely published author, Dr. Warner made comments that were insightful and always right on target.

Saundra Mace, administrative assistant to the chairperson of the Department of Political Science, prepared the camera-ready version of the book. As always, her work was of the highest quality, was timely, and was given generously. Simply put, Saundra is the best.

Dr. Ken Ellinger, friend and colleague, helped obtain some of the data used in the book and provided us with lively discussions on educational politics. This was especially helpful.

We also wish to thank the personnel of the school districts analyzed as case studies. Their cooperation resulted in a vital piece of this book and advances the second generation discrimination literature.

At Greenwood Publishing Group we wish to thank Ms. Jane Garry for accepting the book for publication. Not without controversy, the book advances the proposition that educational policy cannot be separated from the political process. This argument is not a widely shared view among many political scientists and educational scholars. At Greenwood Publishing, Krystyna Budd served as our copyeditor. The book is much better as a result of her careful review. Finally, Mr. David Palmer served as our production editor. We certainly thank David for his support and patience.

Finally, although we would like to take all the credit for all good and blame someone else for any commissions and omissions in the book, we alone are to blame. Please feel free to write Mike to complain.

D.E.W.
M.W.H.
R.E.E.

THE POLITICS OF SECOND GENERATION DISCRIMINATION IN AMERICAN INDIAN EDUCATION

Chapter 1

Introduction

Approximately 90 percent of all American Indian students attend public schools in the United States (Hirschfelder and Kreipe de Montano 1993; Indian Nations at Risk Task Force 1991; Pavel et al. 1995; Swisher 1994a; West 1991). The task of this research is to determine whether these students are receiving equal educational opportunities. Judging from the experiences of African American and Hispanic students, American public schools may not be providing equal educational opportunities for American Indians.

A substantial literature has documented that African American and Hispanic students have been denied access to equal educational opportunities through the use of academic grouping and disciplinary practices (for the most notable studies see Bullock and Stewart 1978, 1979; Eyler, Cook, and Ward 1983; Fraga, Meier, and England 1986; Heller, Holtzman, and Messick 1982; Meier and England 1984; Meier and Stewart 1991; Meier, Stewart, and England 1989; Oakes 1985; Rosenbaum 1976). This issue is of great importance because a school system may remain segregated even after a desegregation plan has been fully implemented. Through the use of common educational practices such as ability grouping and disciplinary measures, minority children may continue to receive different and unequal treatment (Levin and Moise 1975). These resegregative or *"second generation discrimination"* practices have been called "the most invidious kinds of racial discrimination" (Rodgers and Bullock 1972: 69). Not only do the practices "keep schools segregated or resegregate them" (Smith and Dziuban 1977: 52); they also can have an adverse effect on minority students' life chances— "the ability of minority children as adults to participate fully in the social, economic, and political life of society" (Levin 1975: 217). Resegregative policies are labeled second generation discrimination because in theory they occur *after* schools have been desegregated. However, such policies also exist in schools that have not undergone a formal desegregation process. Thus, in some cases the term "second generation discrimination" is misleading.

Despite the impact that second generation school discrimination has on students, systematic, comparative, and empirical research on the topic is sparse and relatively recent (for African Americans see Meier and England 1984; Meier, Stewart, and England 1989; for Hispanics see Fraga, Meier, and England 1986; Meier and Stewart 1991). Research by Meier and his associates addresses many of the limitations of previous second generation discrimination research: The research (1) is limited in terms of generalizability, since it takes the form of case studies (e.g., Metz 1978; Rosenbaum 1976); (2) focuses on only one or perhaps two second generation discrimination practices, usually a single form of ability grouping (see Arnez 1978; Children's Defense Fund 1974); (3) is regional in scope (Stewart 1977); (4) is anecdotal in nature (U.S. Commission on Civil Rights 1977); and/or (5) simply summarizes previous findings (Eyler, Cook, and Ward 1983). Although research by Meier and associates systematically measures the incidence of second generation discrimination, analyses exclusively focus on African American or Hispanic students. Since second generation discrimination has such severe consequences, it should be examined not only for African Americans and Hispanics but also for American Indians.

Generally, the examination of American Indian politics and policies is an area of severe neglect in political science and policy research. Indeed, Wilmer, Melody, and Murdock (1994: 269, 274) state:

The worst kind of elitism is that which ignores other cultures, other peoples, other political or economic systems. By ignoring those who are different, stigmatized as "other," we not only deny their existence, but also recognize no dignity or value in these "others." The discipline of political science has certainly been guilty of such neglect with regard to Native Americans. [We] have largely left the study of native peoples and their political systems [as well as policies affecting them] to sociologists and anthropologists and have, therefore, denied the role that [they] continue to play in the political and economic processes of this country. We cannot expect our political leaders to be sophisticated and educated about Indian politics [and policies] if the discipline of political science is itself ignorant in this area what is at stake, at least partially, is genuine political knowledge, and this *episteme* cannot serve as a function of conquest and exclude a stigmatized "other."

Recently, an "At Risk Task Force" was assembled and received testimony from tribal leaders, parents, teachers, educators, and hundreds of citizens at regional hearings in Alaska, Arizona, Minnesota, Montana, North Carolina, Oklahoma, and Washington. Additionally, thirty-two special sessions with over 500 participants were held at the National Education Association's annual conference in cooperation with the National Advisory Council on Indian Education. One of the outcomes of these activities was a report entitled, *Indian Nations at Risk: An Educational Strategy for Action.* This report includes some of the most recent research on the education of American Indians. Research findings suggest that American Indian students historically have experienced and continue to experience discrimination, racial segregation, low quality education, and a lack of equal educational opportunities (see Charles 1987; Croft 1977; Education Commission of the States 1980; Hirschfelder and Kreipe de Montano 1993; Knutson and McCarthy-Tucker 1993; Meyer 1972; Ogbu 1978, 1986; Pertusati 1988; Prucha 1984; Ryan 1982; Swisher 1994a, 1994b; Swisher and Deyhle 1989; Tonemah 1991; U.S. Senate 1969; West 1990, 1991; Whiteman 1984).

Based on the seminal work by Meier and associates, our research uses a theoretically specified model and a systematic, comparative, and empirical methodology to better understand equal educational opportunities afforded American Indian students. More specifically, the research examines second generation discrimination in 128 American public school districts that have at least 1,000 students and a 5 percent American Indian enrollment. Data are drawn from the *1992 Elementary and Secondary School Civil Rights Survey*, published by the Office for Civil Rights (OCR), located in the Department of Education.

An American Indian (as defined in the Indian Self-Determination and Education Assistance Act) is a person who is a member of an Indian tribe, band, nation, or other organized group or community (including any Alaska Native village, regional, or village corporation as defined or established pursuant to the Alaska Native Claims Settlement Act) that is recognized as eligible for the special programs and services provided by the United States to American Indians because of its members' status as American Indians. According to the U.S. Department of the Interior (1991), however, there is no federal tribal definition that establishes a person's identity as Indian. Government agencies use different criteria for determining who is an Indian. Similarly, tribal groups have varying requirements for determining tribal membership. Therefore, for definitional purposes of this research, American Indians are those who identified themselves as such. This method, also used by the Census Bureau in 1990, is considered to provide the most accurate data obtained on American Indians (Bureau of the Census 1988).

Our research tests three major arguments. First, American Indians may be denied equal educational opportunities through the use of *academic grouping* (which includes ability grouping, special education, and curriculum tracking) and *disciplinary practices*. Academic grouping techniques are often subtle methods of discrimination that allow schools to sort students into homogeneous groups; they allow American Indians and whites to be separated. Ability grouping is used to separate students according to perceived academic potential, with gifted and talented classes offering the highest quality of education and remedial classes providing the lowest quality of education. In American public schools, students are frequently homogeneously grouped into different levels of classes of the same subject.

Special education classes are for students deemed unable to benefit from the normal curriculum. For some (or all) classes, special education students are grouped and separated from students in the normal curriculum. Special education students are further sorted into several different types of classes, including classes for the educable mentally retarded (EMR), trainable mentally retarded (TMR), and the specific learning disabled (LD).

Schools may also use disciplinary actions to keep American Indians from receiving equal educational opportunities and to separate them from their white classmates. The second generation discrimination disciplinary practice we examine is disparities in the number of American Indian students who are suspended from school. Disparities in suspensions based on race can discourage American Indian students from remaining in school.

Additionally, research suggests the presence of a second generation school discrimination disparities "pattern." Based on previous findings for African Americans (see Meier, Stewart, and England 1989), for instance, the pattern that may occur is one in which schools that disproportionately separate American Indian students into lower academic groups may similarly disproportionately subject American Indian students to harsh disciplinary practices (e.g., suspensions). Such a pattern is consistent with a denial of equal educational opportunities for American Indian students.

The second major argument tested is that *political power* is the key to limiting second generation discrimination and to increasing equal educational opportunities for American Indian students. School districts that have greater American Indian political power have greater political representation on the school board. Greater American Indian school board representation in turn leads to greater American Indian representation in the school administration, which in turn leads to larger numbers of American Indian teachers. One of the most important and consistent factors limiting the amount of second generation discrimination American Indian students experience is the presence of American Indian teachers. American Indian representation on school boards occurs in districts where American Indian political resources (e.g., population, income, and education) are higher.

The final argument tested is that the *behavior of street-level bureaucrats* (Lipsky 1980), in this case teachers, *is important in limiting second generation discrimination* and to increasing the equal educational opportunities for American Indian students. This research tests not only whether street-level bureaucrats are important, but it also examines what it is about their behavior (for example, their teaching methods) that may limit the amount of second generation discrimination American Indian students experience.

RESEARCH OUTLINE

Our research addressing second generation discrimination among American Indians is organized into seven additional chapters. Chapter 2 provides a brief overview of the political history of American Indian education and associated issues and problems. Chapter 3 presents a political theory of educational policy. Chapter 4 outlines the data used in the research and discusses variable measurement and operationalization. Chapter 5 introduces our policy indicators of second generation discrimination, measures the incidence of second generation discrimination for academic grouping, discipline, and educational outcomes, and shows how second generation discrimination indicators are interrelated. Based on a theoretically specified model, in chapter 6 second generation discrimination among American Indians is explained.

Chapter 7 presents a discussion of on-site case studies undertaken to better understand the dynamics of second generation discrimination. Specific within-school policies (e.g., grant writing) and practices (e.g., teaching methods) that either facilitate or constrain second generation discrimination are the focus of the case studies. The case studies enrich our overall understanding of second generation discrimination and augment our aggregate data analysis. Finally, chapter 8 summarizes research findings and discusses implications of the study. The chapter closes with suggestions for future research.

Chapter 2

A Political History of American Indian Education

A knowledge of the political history of American Indian education is essential for understanding current problems American Indians face in their pursuit of equal educational opportunities. This chapter outlines the American Indian struggle for equal educational opportunities from the days before American Indians were considered citizens of the U.S. government and state governments to the present. This overview not only provides an important historical background that demonstrates that American Indians have not been afforded equal educational opportunities but also suggests how and why discrimination has occurred.

EARLY AMERICAN INDIAN EDUCATION POLICY: CONSTITUTIONAL UNDERPINNINGS

The federal role in American Indian education has its basis in the treaty and commerce clauses of the U.S. Constitution. More generally, Indian law is codified under Title 25 of the U.S. Code. Article II, Section 2, of the Constitution gives the president the power to make treaties with the advice and consent of two-thirds of the Senate. Article I, Section 8, of the Constitution invests Congress with the authority to regulate commerce with Indian tribes. Until the Indian Appropriation Act of 1871, in accordance with international law, the United States treated Indian tribes as separate nations (see *Worcester v. Georgia* 1832). The president frequently negotiated treaties with specific provisions for education. In fact, between 1778 and 1871, when congressional action ended treaty negotiations with

Indian tribes (Indian Nations at Risk Task Force 1991; U.S. Department of the Interior 1991), provisions for educational services and facilities were included in 120 of the nearly 400 treaties between Indian nations and the federal government (Hirschfelder and Kreipe de Montano 1993; O'Brien 1990a; Swisher 1994a). Promoting education meant encouraging Christian missionary contacts. The U.S. government used the "Civilization Fund," which had established a permanent appropriation for carrying out its educational purposes, as seed money for various Protestant denominations. More importantly, providing education to American Indians meant forced assimilation, although at the time it was considered humanitarianism.

The treaty and commerce clauses overrode what otherwise would have been an impermissible entanglement between church and state as government funds were used to build churches, schools, housing, and grants of land to sectarian missions. Together, the treaty and commerce clauses produced a third plenary power over Indian affairs capable of overriding objections to state-supported sectarian education through "contract" schools. This plenary power was characterized as a guardian-ward relationship, with the United States assuming full responsibility. This trust responsibility has been stated and reaffirmed in numerous government documents, lower court decisions, and Supreme Court decisions (see *Cherokee Nation v. Georgia* 1831; *Seminole Nation v. United States* 1942; *Worcester v. Georgia* 1832).

DECLINE OF THE CHRISTIAN REFORM MOVEMENT AND RISE OF BIA COMMON SCHOOLS

By the end of the 1800s sectarian factionalism put an end to the contract schools. Common schools for American Indians were advocated because such schools represented mainstream North American Protestantism, promoted patriotism, and were utilitarian (Ryan 1982). For American Indians, education changed to include training schools. The guardian-ward relationship was conferred upon the Bureau of Indian Affairs (BIA) school system.

Education and land policies shared the goal of assimilation (Ryan 1982; Sharpes 1979). The General Allotment Act of 1887 (more commonly called the Dawes Severalty Act, named after its chief sponsor Senator Henry Dawes of Massachusetts), for instance, allotted reservation land to individual Indians and opened reservation "surplus land," which was bought by non-Indians. As a result of the Dawes Act, American Indian education changed again, this time to include public school districts that were needed for the children of many non-Indian settlers.

AMERICAN INDIAN EDUCATION AND PUBLIC SCHOOLS

Once American Indians were citizens rather than domestic subjects, they had the constitutional right under state laws to attend public schools. Nevertheless, many public schools were geographically inaccessible to American Indian children. Moreover, *Plessy v. Ferguson* (1896), which upheld the concept of "separate but equal education," also applied to American Indian children in the western states. Thus, many children of American Indian citizens still continued to use BIA common schools.

In 1924 the Indian Citizenship Act was passed. This act conferred citizenship to approximately one-third of the Indian population that had yet to gain citizenship status. Thus, all American Indians became citizens of the United States and the states in which they resided. They were entitled by the Fourteenth Amendment of the Constitution to participate in all federal and state programs, including education, which the states had the primary responsibility for providing.

Although the question of U.S. citizenship for American Indians was settled in 1924, some states still refused to recognize American Indians as citizens of the state in which they resided. State governments refused to grant American Indians basic rights such as equal educational opportunities and the right to vote. American Indians were forced to use litigation to secure voting rights. In 1927, for instance, a federal district court in *Deere v. State* (1927) held that American Indians, being citizens of the United States and residing in a state, were to be held as citizens of the state (McCool 1985). The Arizona Supreme Court reached a similar conclusion the following year in *Porter v. Hall* (1928). However, according to McCool (1985), in 1940 five states still prohibited voting to nontaxed American Indians. In *Trujillo v. Garley* (1948) a federal district court reiterated the *Deere* principle and declared that the Indian pueblos in New Mexico were part of the state: Residents of the pueblos were state residents and had voting rights. In 1956 in Utah, the last state in the United States to permit American Indian voting, the state legislature had to overturn a state court decision (*Allen v. Merrell* 1956) in order for American Indians to be permitted to vote.

Nevertheless, opponents of American Indian voting rights continued to try to disfranchise them (see McCool 1985; *Montoya v. Bolack* 1962; U.S. Department of the Interior 1991) and in some instances managed to keep American Indians from voting in school board elections (Deloria and Lytle 1983; McCool 1985; McDonald 1989). Discrimination in voting rights likely occurred because of the fear whites had of potential American Indian voting and its impact on education policy. This fear was so great that the Utah Supreme Court denied American Indian voting rights in 1956 in *Allen v. Merrell.* This decision was offered despite an Arizona Supreme Court ruling in *Harrison v. Laveen* (1948) that the question of determining what is "good public policy" is for the executive and legislative branches to determine; courts must base their decisions on the law. Fortunately for American Indians, the Utah Supreme Court's decision was overturned and in more recent cases American Indian rights have been upheld. For instance, the New Mexico Supreme Court ruled in *Prince v. Board of Education* (1975) that American Indians may vote on school bond issues even though they are not taxed in order to repay the bond. Similarly, the Arizona Supreme Court ruled that an American Indian may be elected to a county position even though he is immune from county and state taxation (*Shirley v. Superior Court* 1973).

At the beginning of the American Indian struggle for citizenship there were more American Indians enrolled in public schools than in other types of schooling available to American Indians (Hirschfelder and Kreipe de Montano 1993; Prucha 1984; Ryan 1982; Swisher 1994a). Prucha (1984) believes that this was true not because of a policy of integrating American Indians into public schools but in large part because of the poor quality and low numbers of schools maintained by the federal government. In 1927, for example, only six schools existed where an American Indian could receive a high school education. Furthermore, the Meriam Report (1928), which focused on problems associated with government provided schools, revealed such shocking conditions as severe overcrowding and grossly inadequate student care in boarding schools. The schools were partly supported by the labor of children, and teachers were often poorly trained. The report argued that the federal policy goal of American Indian assimilation could be better achieved through public schools and that American Indians should be included in educational decision making.

Following suggestions from the Meriam Report (1928), the government began a new policy in the 1930s that shifted focus away from BIA schools to public schools for American Indian students. During the same time period, more public schools were built in order to meet the needs of the growing white population. Additionally, there was an increasing interest in public schools among American Indian parents. In 1934 Congress responded to this interest and to the increasing number of American Indians attending public schools with passage of the Johnson–O'Malley Act (JOM). This act provided assistance to public school districts for each American Indian student enrolled. Public school officials wanted to collect "lost" funds that could not be generated from American Indians who lived on tax-free lands. Since passage of the Johnson–O'Malley Act, most American Indian reservation children have attended public schools (Stahl 1979).

The JOM program continued the federal government's attempt at assimilation of American Indian children, but in a manner different from earlier education and land policies. The legislation suggested that it was advisable to fit American Indians into the *general public school system* rather than to provide separate schools for them. The earlier "separate schools" policy had foreseen an end to federal support for children of American Indian citizens and had addressed the general unavailability of public schools only with excepting legislation. In contrast, the JOM program did not immediately end federal support, since it was tied to the presence of nontaxable American Indian land within the borders of a school district. As Ryan (1982) so aptly reminds us, however, the government presumed that the historical trend of allotment sales would continue until very little nontaxable land would remain to justify JOM support.

Generally, JOM allowed the federal government to sign contracts with state governments, rather than with the literally thousands of individual school districts as was necessary before the act, for the costs of American Indian students' education in public schools. Additionally, in 1950 new federal legislation was passed to help local school districts bear the burden of federal government American Indian educational policies and to help finance new school construction. American Indian school-related federal funding policies, especially JOM policies, continued to cause controversy over the years (see Glass 1986; *Hergenreter v. Hayden* 1968; *Indian Oasis et al. v. Warner et al.* 1982; *Middletown School Committee v. Board of Regents for Education of Rhode Island* 1977). JOM funds, for instance, have been used to augment general school operations and have allowed non-Indian students to benefit from the increased funding more than American Indian students, the intended beneficiaries of the funding.

It took until 1953 for the federal government to completely realize that integration of American Indian children in public schools would raise their levels of educational attainment as well as assimilate them. For many American Indian families residing in cities this was their first exposure to the public school system. Nevertheless, some American Indians would not attend new public schools because in some areas whites were directly opposed to their admission (Prucha 1984). At the dawn of the civil rights era, many American Indian children still were being denied equal educational opportunities.

AMERICAN INDIAN EDUCATION DURING THE CIVIL RIGHTS ERA

Throughout the 1960s and 1970s, in response to and as part of the civil rights movement, Congress passed a number of laws that required local school officials to create programs for economically disadvantaged students, minority children, and students with special educational needs. These programs included, but were not limited to, Title I of the Elementary and Secondary Education Act (ESEA) of 1965, the Bilingual Education Act of 1968, the Indian Education Act of 1972, and the Education of All Handicapped Children Act of 1975. In regard to American Indians, one of the responsibilities of the ESEA was to serve American Indian children in need of extra skills assistance in reading and math. In other words, ESEA provided remedial programs for American Indians. The federal government felt that it had a responsibility to meet the special educational needs of American Indians.

However, special education classes, including educable mentally retarded and learning disabled classes, as well as compensatory programs for low-income students often require pulling students out of regular classes and results in *de facto* segregation or resegregation (Eyler, Cook, and Ward 1983; Gartner and Lipsky 1987; Kaestle and Smith 1982; Meier, Stewart, and England 1989; Monk 1992). Indeed, implementing Title I of ESEA required an organizational structure for the delivery of services that was independent of the regular school program. Separate personnel structures were developed in school districts and in individual schools. Title I personnel were hired and paid for only with Title I funds and were required by law to work only with Title I students (Kaestle and Smith 1982). Title I classes were segregated from the regular school curriculum. By 1976, for instance, about 70 percent of all Title I students receiving remedial reading were "pulled out" of their classes and physically moved to other areas in order to receive their supplemental instruction (Kaestle and Smith 1982).

THE INDIAN EDUCATION ACT OF 1972: HISTORY, PROGRAMS, AND CURRENT STATUS AND ISSUES

The impetus for the Indian Education Act of 1972 began with the Elementary and Secondary Education Act of 1965. The need for the legislation was reinforced in 1969 when the Senate issued a special committee report on American Indian education. This report was entitled *Indian Education: A National Tragedy, A National Challenge*; it was also known as the Kennedy Report. The report, based on studies done throughout the

1960s, focused on the low levels of educational attainment of American Indians, the general absence of American Indians in the field of education, and the need for supplemental educational services for American Indians. The report found that national policies for educating American Indians were failing by major proportions. The committee was struck with the low quality of virtually every aspect of the schooling available to Indian children— school buildings themselves, course material and books, the attitude of teachers and administrative personnel, the accessibility of the schools, inadequate remedial programs, outmoded and poorly equipped vocational training, and abnormally heavy turnover of the teaching staff.

The committee reached three major conclusions. First, the federal policy of "coercive assimilation" had "disastrous effects" on the education of American Indian children. Next, American Indian students had not been "given educational opportunities anywhere near equal to that offered the great bulk of American children." Finally, a main theme throughout the report was the need for increased American Indian participation in the education of their children. The committee proposed equal-opportunity supplements to basic school operations, as well as a new education act. Many of the report's recommendations were carried out during the Nixon administration with the Indian Education Act of 1972, which was considered by many to be the first major piece of education legislation dealing with American Indians in fifty years (Ryan 1982; Stahl 1979).

The Indian Education Act (IEA) of 1972 is the only piece of equal education opportunity legislation specifically focusing on American Indians. And although the act was passed in 1972, to date no other significant acts have been passed. The programs under the Indian Education Act of 1972 were directed at public schools, where in the early 1970s more than 70 percent of the American Indian school-age population was enrolled. Part A of the act, also known as the Indian Elementary and Secondary School Assistance Act, provided assistance to local education agencies in order to establish programs meeting the special needs of American Indian students. Some of these programs include health and nutritional services, remedial instruction, and vocational instruction. Additionally, education amendments in 1974 and 1978 authorized the funding of special education programs designed to provide equal educational opportunities for American Indian children.

Part B of the act provided funds for special programs and projects to improve American Indian educational opportunities. This component focused on research, demonstration projects, and educational service projects that could develop appropriate bilingual and curriculum materials for use by local education agencies. The government assumed the responsibility for producing American Indian teachers, school administrators, and other educational professionals. This provision of the act was seen as critical in light of the fact that very few American Indian teachers existed. Only 1.0 percent of American Indian students were taught by American Indian teachers. Moreover, one-fourth of all elementary and secondary teachers by their own admission preferred *not* to teach American Indian students (U.S. Senate 1969).

Part C of the act established special programs for adult American Indians, mostly for improved literacy opportunities and skills development. Finally, part D was primarily administrative in nature and called for an Office of Indian Education within the U.S. Office of Education, a deputy commissioner of Indian Education, and a National Advisory Council for Indian Education with responsibility for recommending a deputy commissioner to advise the U.S. Commissioner of Education, Congress, and the president on Indian education issues.

Ryan (1982) asserts that the conscious decision not to place Indian Education Act programs within the Bureau of Indian Affairs reflected a widely held congressional view that the organizing principle should be education, not the management of resources and American Indian people. Another important reason for placing the Indian Education Act programs within the Office of Education had to do with eligibility differences between the BIA and IEA programs. Most BIA programs limit eligibility to members of federally recognized American Indian tribes with at least one-quarter Indian blood living on or near a federal Indian reservation, whereas IEA programs provide education assistance to all federally recognized American Indians whether or not they are on or near reservations. The Indian Education Act addresses itself to all American Indians, including urban Indians, members of terminated tribes, and other non-federal Indians. The act recognizes that a responsibility exists on the part of the federal government to provide educational assistance to all American Indians.

Although the Office of Indian Education in 1990 funded 1,153 programs in forty-two states serving the special education needs of over 354,000 elementary and secondary American Indian students (Hirschfelder and Kreipe de Montano 1993), how effective IEA programs have been in promoting equal educational opportunity is very questionable. States have used the special political relationship between tribes and the federal government as an excuse for not honoring their responsibilities to American Indians as citizens. As a result, states have not fully provided services (Indian Nations at Risk Task Force 1991).

Moreover, in at least one important respect, the Indian Education Act of

Table 2.1
American Indian Enrollment by School Type

School Type	1914	1952	1961	1971	1978	1990
Federal/	32,698	46,681	47,759	59,289	56,000	49,534
Other	(56.5)	(46.8)	(42.4)	(36.3)	(20.7)	(12.9)
Public	25,180	52,960	64,987	103,885	215,000	333,494
	(43.5)	(53.2)	(57.6)	(63.7)	(79.3)	(87.1)

Note: This table reports raw numbers and percentages (in parentheses).

Sources:
  1914—Prucha, Francis Paul. 1984. *The Great Father: The United States Government and the American Indians, Volumes 1 & 2.* Lincoln, NE: University of Nebraska Press.
  1952, 1961, and 1971—U.S. Department of the Interior, Bureau of Indian Affairs. *Statistics Concerning Indian Education.* Washington, D.C.: Branch of Education, Bureau of Indian Affairs. Issues for 1952, 1961, 1971.
  1978—Robert J. Havighurst. 1981. "Indian Education: Accomplishments of the Last Decade." *Phi Delta Kappan* 62: 5 (January): 329.
  1990—National Advisory Council on Indian Education. 1990. *Toward the Year 2000: Listening to the Voice of Native America, 17th Annual Report to the U.S. Congress.* Washington, D.C.: The Council.

1972 is similar to the Elementary and Secondary Education Act of 1965. Both acts created many "special" programs to meet the special needs of students. According to Meier, Stewart, and England (1989), these programs helped to cause and institutionalize much of the second generation discrimination found today in American public schools. While some of this discrimination is surely intentional, a great deal of the discrimination is unintentional and is the result of the cross-pressures of public education policies. On the one hand, federal policy is to integrate and educate American Indians in the public schools. On the other hand, compensatory educational policies such as special education or programs for economically and educationally disadvantaged children may cause these students to be pulled out of regular classrooms, which may result in segregation, resegregation, and second generation discrimination. Much of the remainder of this book measures the incidence of second generation discrimination for American Indians in a large number of U.S. school districts, explains this incidence using a theoretical model, and offers mitigating strategies to address the serious consequences of second generation discrimination.

educational policymaking is used to examine school district policies of academic grouping, discipline, and access to equal educational opportunities.

We begin the chapter with a brief discussion of the importance of education and an argument that educational policymaking is a political process. Viewing educational policymaking as a political process involves using a theory of representational politics. This theory argues that American Indians must gain access to political and administrative policymaking positions in order to affect educational policies directed at American Indian students. Thus, American Indian representation is included in our theory of policymaking, along with American Indian political resources, social class pressures, ethnic competition, and school district size.

THE IMPORTANCE OF EDUCATION AND EQUAL ACCESS

"Of all the forums for discrimination, discrimination in education is the most invidious" (Meier and Stewart 1991: 2). It is likely that the single best indicator of discrimination in other areas is previous discrimination in education. Equal access to education is important because of the multiple outcomes that education can produce. There are two types of benefits from education, private and social. Private benefits from education include enhanced income earnings and better job opportunities (Cohn 1979). For instance, based on 1992 U.S. Bureau of the Census statistics, as a person gains more education, he or she also gains more income (but see Jencks et al. 1972). Statistics reveal that a person with a high school education will make almost $12,000 a year more than someone without a high school education. Additionally, someone with a college education will make almost $20,000 a year more than someone with a high school education.

The linkage between education and income is not new. The "human capital approach" to economics can be traced back to research in the early 1960s. For example, in 1961 Schultz argued that the main determinant of a person's income was the person's education. More recently, Duncan (1984) offers similar sentiments. He finds that long-term differences in an individual's earnings are accounted for by different levels of education. Education alone explained 15 percent of the variation in income, which was five times the magnitude attributable to any other factor, including achievement, motivation, father's education, personal efficacy, test scores, and work experience.

Education can also generate private benefits for individuals by increasing their access to certain types of jobs. Levin (1975) argues that the type of educational tracks students are provided determines future job opportunities. Students tracked into lower-level classes are not able to gain prestigious job positions. These students are usually put in the lower echelon of the job hierarchy. Therefore, schools inevitably help determine the fate of students by giving them or denying them access to equal education. In short, education not only increases a person's income but also improves access to specific types of jobs, especially professional jobs, such as accountants, doctors, and lawyers.

Another private benefit that results from education involves educational attainment, which is seen as the key to upward mobility (Cohen and Tyree 1986). Research emphasizes that education has the most influence in allowing intergenerational escapes from poverty. The effect of education is greatest for the poor. In this sense, education may be even more critical for American Indians than any other minority group, since they represent the most economically disadvantaged group in the United States (O'Brien 1990b; Tippeconnic 1991; Yates 1987). This is especially the case with respect to poverty and unemployment rates (Johnson 1992; McQuiston and Brod 1984; O'Brien 1990b; Yates 1987). Almost 28 percent of all American Indians live below the poverty level, compared to 12.4 percent for the nation as a whole (Johnson 1992). The overall unemployment rate among American Indians is at least 40 percent (Yates 1987). Furthermore, the mean household income for American Indians is $15,418, compared to $21,173 for whites (Reyhner 1992).

Another way of looking at the private benefits received from education is to analyze the relationship between education and income for American Indians in the school districts used in this study. Using the percentage of American Indians with a high school diploma to predict average American Indian income, Table 3.1 shows a strong positive relationship. Education alone explains 14 percent of the variation in American Indian incomes across the school districts.

Although many of the benefits derived from education have positive benefits for the individual, positive impacts can also be accrued by society as a whole. These benefits, which often go ignored, are termed social benefits. They include, although are not limited to, a more talented and productive workforce (Cohn 1979), more coproduction or volunteerism in the delivery of services (Connelly and Wright 1993), greater political socialization (Sleeter and Grant 1985), and better citizenship (Schultz 1963).

In sum, education is increasingly seen by many to be one of the keys, if not *the* key, to solving such problems as crime, unemployment, welfare dependency, and other socioeconomic ills (Burtless 1987; Henig 1985; Kozol 1985; Murray 1984). Education is the major factor affecting a person's life chances—the ability of one to participate fully in political, social, and

Table 3.1
Impact of American Indian Education on American Indian Income (N=128)

Dependent Variable: American Indian Income

Independent Variable	Unstandarized Regression Coefficients	Standard Errors
Am. Indians With High School Diploma (%)	$143.83**	32.05
Constant	$4,317.32	680.97

R^2 = .14
F = 20.14

** p<.01

economic life (Heidenheimer, Heclo, and Adams 1990; Meier, Stewart, and England 1989).

THE POLITICS OF EDUCATION

The belief that the public education process is apolitical has enjoyed impressive and long lasting popularity with the general public and among scholars (but see Meier, Stewart, and England 1989, 1991; Wirt and Kirst 1989). Significant political reforms in educational policy began in the early 1900s. These reforms, and most reforms since then, were intended to insulate schools, especially in urban areas, from the influence of politics (see Bierlein 1993; Lineberry and Fowler 1967; Spring 1993; Tyack 1974; Wirt and Kirst 1989). Much of the research focusing on urban service delivery, including education tends to argue that politics seldom matters (see D. Wright 1992; for exceptions see Meier, Stewart, and England 1991). Instead, the common understanding is that urban services, including education, are distributed according to bureaucratic decision rules that result in "unpatterned inequalities."

Even research on equal access to education has been described "as though it were outside any political framework" (Weinberg 1983: 333). After examining previous research on educational policy, Meier, Stewart, and England (1989) conclude that the dominant ideology is that politics has no impact on educational policies. They argue that reforms that separated school districts from city politics succeeded in insulating schools from the influence of local partisan politics, but the reforms did not eliminate politics from the school system. In other words, politics—the authoritative allocation of values (Easton 1965) or who gets what and how (Lasswell 1936)—still exist, it just may not be of a partisan nature. School board members specifically and school personnel more generally are required to make decisions regarding the allocation of public tax dollars and other important education services. In short, political power is important, and the lack of political power may be seen as a main cause of unequal access to education (Olivas 1983).

In order for American Indians to influence educational policymaking, past research (Meier and Stewart 1991; Meier, Stewart, and England 1989) suggests, they must be able to influence three key decisions, which are dominated by three different groups of decision makers. The first decision is the determination of the overall school district policy, which is determined by the school board. The next decision involves translating the overall policy into administrative rules and procedures and is dominated by the school district administration. Finally, the third decision is the application of the rules and procedures to individual students, which is clearly left up to teachers.

The best way for American Indians to influence educational policymaking may be to place representatives into school board, administrative, and teaching positions, which involves the notion of a representative bureaucracy (see Kingsley 1944; Levitan 1946; Long 1952; Meier 1975; Mosher 1968, 1982; Saltzstein 1979). A bureaucracy is representative, at least in the passive sense, if bureaucrats share the same demographic origins, that is, ethnicity, race, gender, religion, education, and so on, as the general population they serve. In this sense, a bureaucracy is perceived as less of a threat to democracy if the bureaucracy is representative of all interests in society (Mosher 1982; Redford 1969). Furthermore, the bureaucracy is seen as less threatening if it mirrors the social origins of the population because they share the population's socialization experiences, have similar attitudes, and make policy decisions similar to those that the populace would make if it participated in all decisions. Additionally, a representative bureaucracy view of educational policymaking emphasizes that all three groups of decision makers have some degree of discretion in the decisions they make; thus, American Indians in these positions could use their discretion to increase the access of American Indian students to equal educational opportunities.

The discretion that the three groups of decision makers possess are in different areas. School board members are limited by certain legal and ethical constraints (e.g., conflict of interest). Additionally, they are constrained by the budgets of their school districts. Nonetheless, school board members still have substantial amounts of discretion and will likely use this discretion to maximize their own policy preferences. In accordance with the representative bureaucracy argument, for example, it is expected that an American Indian elected to the school board will favor policies that benefit American Indian students. Although an American Indian board member might on occasion try overtly to influence or pass policies beneficial to American Indians, on a day-to-day basis he or she will probably be more likely to support the hiring of American Indian administrators who vigorously support the concept of equal educational opportunity.

Research examining the topic of bureaucratic discretion (Downs 1967; Meier 1987; Rourke 1984) suggests that it is virtually impossible for elected policymakers, such as school board members, to make policies that leave no discretion to administrators. In fact, because of bureaucratic expertise and numerous other sources of bureaucratic power, elected officials often defer decisions to the bureaucratic organization (Meier 1987; Rourke 1984). Even if this deferral is not offered, agency officials can change legislative intent in the process of implementing policies (for examples see Bullock and Lamb 1984; Goggin et al. 1990; Meier 1987). The assumption is that similar to school board members, administrators will maximize their own policy preferences by exercising their bureaucratic discretion.

Principals as school building administrators find themselves in a loosely defined hierarchy. Although they have discretion, they also need to maintain credibility and trust with the central administration and school board members (Burlingame 1986; Crowson and Morris 1985; Wirt and Kirst 1989). Often principals' discretionary power is limited in budgetary matters (Bridges 1982). Principals may also exercise varying amounts of discretion depending on how they view their representational role, either as "trustees" to make decisions based on their own judgment or as "delegates" to seek out a collective opinion from faculty, staff, and/or students (see Mann 1976).

At the so-called street level of educational bureaucracies are teachers. Teachers have a high degree of autonomy in choosing how they will implement policy because much of what they do occurs in isolation—"hidden behind classroom doors" (Cohen 1982: 488). Teachers not only implement policy; they also develop or make educational policy. Teachers as street-level bureaucrats (Lipsky 1980) are important because they have the opportunity to observe the children in the classroom setting and to see them working on challenging problems. Most often teachers get to make the *first* judgment about a child's cognitive ability and whether to refer a child for psychological testing. Teachers also determine to a large extent the type of teaching that is performed, for example, memorization, pencil-and-paper exercises, hands-on learning, computer-aided instruction, current events, and/or cooperative learning methods.

Some researchers characterize teachers as "political brokers" who enjoy considerable discretion (Bickel 1982; Schwille, Porter, and Gant 1980; Wirt and Kirst 1989). In this sense, teachers are rational decision makers who calculate the costs and benefits of exercising their discretion in order to pursue their own policy preferences. Most teachers can allocate public resources by exercising their discretion in matters such as determining which curriculum students receive, recommending placement in various academic groups, using discipline, and encouraging or discouraging students (Bickel 1982; Cummins 1992; McIntyre 1990; Soodak and Podell 1993; Weick 1976; Wirt and Kirst 1989).

Much of the preceding discussion suggests an organizational structure for American public schools that is characterized by "loose coupling" (Cibulka 1991; Wieck 1976). With this type of organizational structure each group of decision makers has autonomy within its own realm of expertise. For example, the behavior of teachers or the teaching methods used within classrooms are under weak formal control from administrators. Thus, most teachers have a great deal of discretion with regard to how they teach and/or how they treat students. As a result, teachers are hypothesized to have a greater impact on second generation discrimination than administrators or school board members. Similarly, administrators are seldom constrained by school board members, in hiring decisions, when dealing with students who end up in the principal's office, and in implementing policies set by the school board. Finally, teachers and school building administrators have little control over determining broad school district policies; instead these decisions are left up to the school board.

In sum, this research seeks to determine whether American Indian access to these three groups of decision-making positions, where school board members, administrators, and teachers have discretionary power to seek their own personal policy preferences, results in educational policies that benefit American Indian students (see Kirksey and Wright 1992; Lineberry 1978). The research does not directly measure policy preferences; instead it uses race as a surrogate measure of policy preferences (see Meier and Stewart 1991; Meier, Stewart, and England 1989, 1991; Polinard, Wrinkle, and Longoria 1990). This is justifiable for several reasons. First, race is a demographic characteristic that is especially salient. Moreover, research has shown that race and ethnicity is one of the best predictors of policy preferences or political attitudes and that policy preferences vary by race and ethnicity (see Lovrich 1974; Lovrich and Taylor 1976). Additionally, of all the demographic surrogates for individual values or policy preferences, ethnicity or race is the strongest and longest lasting (Free and Cantril 1967). Finally, the arguments associated with a representative bureaucracy also justify the use of race. Consequently, it is assumed that American Indian school board members, administrators, and teachers favor policies that provide greater equal educational opportunities for American Indian students and oppose policies that reduce or limit the access to quality education for American Indian students.

A THEORY OF REPRESENTATIONAL POLITICS

Our theory of representational roles and American Indian education builds on the work of Meier, Stewart, and England (1989) for African Americans and Meier and Stewart (1991) for Hispanics. The theory assumes that American Indian school board members, administrators, and teachers mitigate the impact of second generation discrimination on American Indian students.

School board members, school administrators, and teachers are selected using different methods. In most districts, school board members are elected. Administrators are usually hired by school boards or by other upper-level administrators. Teachers are usually hired by school administrators using merit criteria. Although the selection procedures are different, a similar political theory can be used to explain American Indian access to each of these positions. Our theory of representational politics changes slightly for each set of decision makers and is based on three different groups of political variables: American Indian political resources (including population and education), social class, and American Indian access to other decision-making positions, beginning with school board seats.

Access to School Board Seats

American Indian Political Resources
In order for American Indians to influence policy outcomes, they must capture seats on the school board (see Barlow 1984; Lutz and Barlow 1980, 1981). One necessary, although certainly not sufficient, political resource is American Indian votes or population.[1] Furthermore, it is imperative for American Indians to vote as a bloc in order to influence elections (Engstrom and Barrilleaux 1991; McCool 1985; McCoy 1992). American Indians have been prevented from voting (see McCool 1985 for a comprehensive effort analyzing American Indian voting; Svingen 1992) using many of the methods used against other minorities, including English

literacy tests, legislative apportionment, white primaries, poll taxes (*Little Thunder v. South Dakota* 1975), gerrymandering, and state residency requirements (Deloria and Lytle 1983; McCool 1985; *Montoya v. Bolack* 1962; U.S. Department of the Interior 1991). Moreover, in some instances American Indians have even been prevented from voting in school board elections (Deloria and Lytle 1983; Engstrom and Barrilleaux 1991; McCool 1985; McDonald 1989).

An additional requirement needed for American Indians to win elections is credible American Indian candidates (Engstrom and Barrilleaux 1991; McDonald 1989). Meier, Stewart, and England (1989) and Meier and Stewart (1991) suggest that ethnic groups produce viable candidates for political office once the ethnic group contains members who are middle class. This also seems to be the case for American Indians (see Barlow 1984; Gross 1989; McCool 1985). For example, increased economic prosperity for the Coeur d'Alene American Indian tribe resulted in viable American Indian political candidates and eventually elected officials (Barlow 1984). Two accepted middle-class resource measures are education and income. Middle-class status for American Indians is measured using the percentage of American Indians with high school diplomas. Income is another typical measure of middle class status. We use income in our model, but it is used to indicate both social class and the "power thesis" of intergroup relations (see below).

Social Class
The power theory of intergroup relations, also referred to as the "conflict approach" or "competitive ethnicity" (see Blalock 1967; Blumer 1958; Schermerhorn 1956; Wilson 1973), views relationships among groups as a function of their competitive positions in political, economic, and social arenas (Feagin 1980; Giles and Evans 1985, 1986; Giles and Hertz 1994). The larger the social differences among the different groups, the more magnified the competition and conflict.

Giles and Evans (1985, 1986) argue that if a minority group is similar to the majority with respect to social class characteristics, the majority will be less threatened by the demands of the minority. Similarly, if the size of a minority group is not large enough to pose significant competition to the majority, the minority group can expect better treatment by the majority (Blalock 1967). Discrimination is more likely when the social differences among groups are large. Conversely, discrimination is less likely against middle-class minority groups than against lower-class minority groups, since middle-class minority groups share many of the same values as middle-class whites (Giles and Evans 1986). Feagin (1980) presents a parallel argument. He argues that second generation discrimination is highly related to the socioeconomic status of whites, in which case middle- and upper-level whites are the strongest opponents of integration and desegregation. Thus, it seems that class has as much to do with discrimination as does race.

American Indian education is one indicator of American Indian social class, but educational attainment is already being used as an indicator of American Indian political resources. However, as Meier, Stewart, and England (1989) note, if a fundamental cause of discrimination is social class, then such discrimination is as likely to affect poor whites as it is to affect poor African Americans, or in our case poor American Indians. Thus, political institutions of the majority are likely to deny access to poor whites as well as to poor American Indians. Likewise, in a community with a large number of poor whites, the political resources of the middle-class white community will be mobilized against the lower-class white community. In such a situation, American Indians, especially those who are middle-class, may be more acceptable to the middle-class white community. This social-class power thesis aspect of representational politics is measured by the percentage of the white community that resides in poverty. This variable should be positively related to American Indian school board representation.

Access to Administrative Positions

Previous research has demonstrated the beneficial role of minority administrators for African Americans (Meier, Stewart, and England 1989), Hispanics (Meier and Stewart 1991), Mexican Americans (Polinard, Wrinkle, and Longoria 1990), and Latinos (Meier 1993). In contrast, the policy impact of American Indian school administrators has not been evaluated, although research shows that American Indian leaders of some organizations play a significant role in policymaking (Gross 1989; McCoy 1992). Instead, most of the studies on American Indian representation in administrative positions stress a patronage argument and to a lesser degree a representative bureaucracy argument. The patronage argument is that American Indians should have the same share of administrative positions that they have of the population or that they have of the school district (see Indian Nations at Risk Task Force 1991; Jones and Montenegro 1982; Lynch and Charleston 1990; Noley 1992; Tippeconnic 1991). Such a distribution would be consistent with notions of fairness and equity (see Dye and Renick 1981; Mladenka 1989a). The representative bureaucracy view of equity stresses the discretion of administrative officials. Rourke (1984) points out that administrators, like elected officials, frequently exercise discretion. Thus, an American Indian administrator is assumed to be more likely to make decisions that benefit other American Indians.

American Indian School Board Members

American Indian access to administrative positions uses the same model of political representation as the school board seat model discussed above with one exception. The percentage of American Indian school board members in a district is added to the American Indian administrative positions political model of representation. Districts with a higher percentage of African American school board members employ a larger percentage of African American school administrators (Meier, Stewart, and England 1989). Similar findings are found for Hispanics (Meier and Stewart 1991) and Mexican Americans (Polinard, Wrinkle, and Longoria 1990). A parallel finding should exist for American Indians. Previous second generation discrimination literature suggests this parallel finding for two reasons. First, the school district superintendent is hired by the school board. The school board can either choose an American Indian for the position or employ a person who strongly supports American Indian hiring (see Barlow 1984; Lutz and Barlow 1981; Spring 1993; Wirt and Kirst 1989). Second, the school board can establish an affirmative action policy for lower-level administrative positions or apply informal pressure on higher-level administrators to hire (or promote) more American Indian administrators.

American Indian Resources

Meier, Stewart, and England (1989) argue that resources (education and population) influence school administrative hiring in two ways. First, they function as political resources. That is, they are surrogates for the American Indian community's political clout, and they measure the ability of American Indians to pressure the school district for favorable policies. Second, they represent favorable labor-pool characteristics. School districts in which the American Indian population is greater and more educated should have more American Indian individuals who are qualified to be school administrators (Indian Nations at Risk Task Force 1991; Jones and Montenegro 1982; Lynch and Charleston 1990; Noley 1992; O'Brien 1990b).

Social Class

The power theory of intergroup relations again predicts that majority white communities would prefer American Indian administrators from middle-class backgrounds, rather than lower-class white administrators.

Furthermore, "the percentage of the white population living in poverty also represents a labor-pool constraint" (Meier, Stewart, and England 1989; Meier and Stewart 1991). School districts with more whites in poverty have fewer qualified white candidates for school board positions, and similarly these districts will have fewer qualified white candidates for administrative positions. This in turn should generate more opportunity for American Indians, especially those with middle incomes.

Access to Teaching Positions

American Indian Administrators

The representation model used for American Indian administrators is also used in the analysis of American Indian teachers with one exception: The influence of American Indian administrators is also considered. Research on public employment shows that administrators frequently hire individuals with characteristics similar to their own (Mladenka 1989a, 1989b; Meier 1993). Put differently, minority employment outcomes are determined by, among other factors, minority administrators in key decision-making positions (Kerr and Mladenka 1994). Research focusing specifically on education has found that administrators also hire individuals with characteristics similar to their own. This was the case for African Americans (Meier, Stewart, and England 1989), Hispanics (Meier and Stewart 1991), and Mexican Americans (Polinard, Wrinkle, and Longoria 1990), and it is believed to be the case for American Indians, although the relationship has not been empirically examined (Noley 1992). Therefore, it is expected that a positive relationship will exist between a school district's percentage of American Indian administrators and its percentage of American Indian teachers.

Previous research by Meier, Stewart, and England (1989) for African Americans and Meier and Stewart (1991) for Hispanics includes minority administrators in the model to help explain African American and Hispanic access to teaching positions, but both studies delete minority school board membership to predict the presence of minority teachers. The argument is that school board members in large urban school districts have only an indirect role in hiring teachers. Since most of the school districts in this sample are not large urban ones, we argue that school board members may have a role in hiring teachers. Indeed, school board members interviewed in our case studies discussed later in the book assert that they had some influence on the hiring decisions of teachers (see also Lutz and Barlow 1981). Thus, in contrast to past research on second generation discrimination, American Indian school board membership is used to explain the presence of American Indian teachers in our school districts.

American Indian Resources

Large American Indian populations and educated American Indian populations should function as they did in regard to administrative positions. Their impact should be twofold. First, they operate as political resources that allow the American Indian community to place pressure on the school district to hire more American Indian teachers. Second, these two resources represent favorable labor-pool characteristics, which increases the pool of American Indian teaching candidates.

Social Class

The power theory of intergroup relations predicts that the white community would prefer American Indian teachers with middle-class backgrounds over white teachers with lower-class backgrounds. Furthermore, a large amount of white poverty means there is an unfavorable pool for recruiting white teachers. This should also help in the attraction of American Indian teachers.

IMPACT OF REPRESENTATION ON EQUAL EDUCATIONAL OPPORTUNITIES

Studies show that minority representation leads to positive policy consequences for minority groups. Meier, Stewart, and England (1989) find that African American representation on school boards leads to the hiring of more African American administrators, which in turn results in the hiring of more African American teachers. Higher numbers of African American teachers leads to less second generation discrimination for African American students. Analogous findings are found by Meier and Stewart (1991) for Hispanics. Research by Polinard, Wrinkle, and Longoria (1990) reports results similar to findings by Meier and associates, but the researchers also find that the effects of Mexican American teachers interact with the effects of Mexican American school board members. More specifically, Mexican American teachers limit second generation discrimination for Mexican American students, but the interaction effect between these teachers and board members even further limits second generation discrimination.

Our theory of representational politics poses the following question: Does passive representation of American Indians in educational bureaucracies result in active representation for American Indian students in educational policies? That is, does American Indian representation have positive impacts on public policy, in this case equal educational opportunities for American

Indian students? Previous studies suggest that three conditions need to exist in order for passive representation to be linked to active representation (see Meier 1993; Meier and Nigro 1976; Meier and Stewart 1991; Meier, Stewart, and England 1989; Saltzstein 1979, 1983; Thompson 1976, 1978). First, the descriptive characteristic in question must be salient, such as ethnicity or race. Research has shown that race or ethnicity is one of the best predictors of political attitudes and that policy preferences vary by race and ethnicity (see Lovrich 1974; Lovrich and Taylor 1976). Second, individual bureaucrats need to have discretion to act. For this research, teachers, as street-level bureaucrats, must have sufficient discretion to make decisions. Finally, policy decisions made by the bureaucracy must be directly relevant to the salient descriptive characteristic of the passively represented. In this case, school district policy decisions regarding American Indian students must be relevant to the American Indians in the community.

A long-standing goal of American Indians has been and continues to be gaining equal access to quality education. Recently, there is a growing movement among organizations representing American Indians that stresses the need for quality education. Some of the more prominent organizations include the National Indian Education Association, the National Advisory Council on Indian Education, and the Native American Rights Fund. Furthermore, American Indians continue to lead events such as the Indian Nations at Risk Task Force held in 1991, the White House Conference on Indian Education held in 1992, and the American Indian Education Summit in 1994, which unify their voices and reinforce their demands for equal access to quality education (Swisher 1994a). Consequently, the policies examined in this research are policies that should be apparent, important, and well understood by American Indian representatives.

The policy area this research addresses is American Indian student access to equal educational opportunity, in which students are treated equally regardless of race. Moreover, equal educational opportunity does not mean assimilation, as it did previously for American Indian students; rather, it is a process that involves a mixing of students that produces intergroup interactions and involves issues of equity (Pettigrew 1991, 1994).

Equal educational opportunities, however, can be restricted by a variety of actions that segregate or resegregate classrooms. Most overt methods of segregation have been eliminated (but see McDonald 1989 on the overt methods of segregation used against American Indians), but more subtle institutional methods of segregation may be used. Such methods include second generation discrimination practices, which are the focus of this research. Second generation discrimination involves the use of academic grouping and discipline, which allows schools to limit interracial contact and deny minority students access to the best quality of education available in a school district (see Bullock and Stewart 1978, 1979; Eyler, Cook, and Ward 1983; Gartner and Lipsky 1987; Heller, Holtzman, and Messick 1982; Hochschild 1984; Meier and Stewart 1991; Meier, Stewart, and England 1989; Oakes 1985; Ogbu 1978; Polinard, Wrinkle, and Longoria 1990). The specific policies we analyze are academic grouping, discipline, and educational attainment.

ACADEMIC GROUPING

Ability grouping, tracking, special education, and other forms of academic grouping gained popularity in the United States in the early 1900s, especially in the 1920s, along with a dramatic increase in the number of students in U.S. schools (see Mecca 1992). Today, academic grouping techniques are prevalent in most school districts (Artiles and Trent 1994; Braddock and Dawkins 1993; Gartner and Lipsky 1987; Mecca 1992; Oakes 1985). Recently, Oakes (1985), in a representative study of junior and senior high schools, determined that over 90 percent of the schools in the sample practiced some variant of tracking, with similar levels existing for elementary schools. Furthermore, at each subsequent grade level more and more students are affected by academic grouping, up to the point where virtually all students are affected.

Typically, students are sorted into three broad categories—honors or gifted, regular or basic, and special education—based on perceived and/or measured intellectual ability and to some degree, at the high school level, career aspirations (Mecca 1992; Oakes 1985). Ability grouping is more common at the elementary school level, whereas curriculum tracking occurs most often at the secondary school level. Meier, Stewart, and England (1989: 23) explain, "Students who the school cannot sort into the various ability groups or tracks within the regular academic program may be classified as 'special' or 'exceptional' and placed in separate special education classes." Put differently, children judged unable to benefit from regular classes are sorted into several different types of special education classes, including the educable mentally retarded (EMR) and the specific learning disabilities (LD). These classes provide help or benefits for the student's "special needs" (Artiles and Trent 1994; Gartner and Lipsky 1987; Gottlieb et al. 1994; Heller, Holtzman, and Messick 1982).

Although academic grouping techniques have been used since the early 1900s, they are not used without controversy, especially in light of increasing research that has documented that minority students can be denied access to equal educational opportunities through such academic grouping practices (Bullock and Stewart 1978, 1979; Eyler, Cook, and Ward 1983; Heller, Holtzman, and Messick 1982; Meier and Stewart 1991; Meier, Stewart, and England 1989; Oakes 1985; Polinard, Wrinkle, and Longoria 1990). Although previous research on second generation discrimination does not analyze American Indians, we argue that the sorting effect of academic grouping may separate white students from American Indians and segregate the school system.

The quality of instruction that special education students receive has also come under fire. The argument is that the education received is inferior because of a "dumbing down" or "watered-down" curriculum (Gartner and Lipsky 1987). Several researchers report that the least experienced and least capable teachers may teach the lowest grouped students—the group that may be the most challenging to teach (Braddock and Dawkins 1993; Finley 1984; Gamoran 1992; Gartner and Lipsky 1987; Mecca 1992; Schafer and Olexa 1971). These researchers contend that the result is a weaker, less challenging learning environment for students in the lower tracks, which leads to unequal educational opportunities by denying them access to the best education the district has to offer. As the controversy over academic grouping has increased, Meier, Stewart, and England (1989) and Meier and Stewart (1991) argue that it seems to center around several issues, including the biases in standardized tests used for grouping, the links that grouping has to discrimination, the conflict grouping has with integration, and the effectiveness of grouping.

Biases in Standardized Tests Used for Academic Grouping

Placement of students into academic groups is determined by student performance on standardized tests, by grades, and by teacher reports. Although researchers as far back as George Sanchez in 1934 have pointed out the inherent biases in IQ tests, classification systems have relied heavily on IQ tests to group students (Artiles and Trent 1994; Cummins 1984, 1986, 1989, 1992; Gottlieb et al. 1994; Smith 1983). For example, a review of academic grouping programs using EMR (educable mentally retarded) classes reveals that IQ tests are the major determinant used to assign students to EMR classes (Bickel 1982, see also Mercer 1982). Use of IQ tests and other psychological tests for educational classification often leads to discriminatory placements of minority groups (Braddock and Dawkins 1993; Cummins 1984, 1986, 1989; Meier and Stewart 1991; Meier, Stewart, and England 1989, 1991; Reschly 1981), including American Indians (Braddock and Dawkins 1993; Cummins 1992; Indian Nations at Risk Task Force

1991; Johnson 1992; Reschly 1978; Reyhner 1992a, 1992b; Yates 1987). These classification systems label a disproportionately large number of minority students as intellectually subnormal and a disproportionately small number as gifted. This is particularly true for gifted and talented American Indian students who are not participating in gifted and talented programs in numbers proportionate to their participation in the larger society (Chinn and Hughes 1987; Florey and Tafoya 1988; Hillabrant et al. 1992; Knutson and McCarthy-Tucker 1993; Ramirez and Johnson 1988; Robbins 1991; Shutiva 1991; Tonemah 1991).

The reasons for exclusion and underrepresentation are unclear, although research suggests many reasons are related to problems with biased standardized testing. For example, greater weight is placed on the verbal, usually English, performance in the interpretation of test scores (Florey and Tafoya 1988; Yates 1987). Standardized tests, which are timed, reward speed (Knutson and McCarthy-Tucker 1993). Additionally, the translations of standardized tests into different languages often do not make sense to the student taking the test because of inadequate translation or because no comparable question in the given language exists (Brescia and Fortune 1988). Furthermore, usually a narrow definition of giftedness is used that reflects a middle-class white culture (Bruch 1975; Johnson 1992; Maker 1983; Tonemah 1987, 1991). Similarly, standardized tests used to identify the gifted are often based on populations that do not include a representative sample from all racial, ethnic, and cultural groups (Johnson 1992; Masten 1981; Padilla and Wyatt 1983; Reschly 1978; Reschly, Kicklighter, and McKee 1988; Rhodes 1989; Shutiva 1991; see Cummins 1989, 1992; Mercer 1973; Oakes 1985 for other examples of the misuse of standardized tests). In short, research finds that currently normed vocational interest tests, psychological tests, and IQ tests are inappropriate and unreliable when administered to American Indian students (Brophy and Aberle 1966; Hulburt, Schulz, and Eide 1985; Johnson 1992; Reschly 1987; Reyhner 1992a).

Biased tests are not the only method of assigning students to academic groups (McIntyre 1990; Meier, Stewart, and England 1989). As mentioned earlier, teachers as street-level bureaucrats, as well as counselors, school psychologists, and administrators, have great discretion in making subjective judgments about the placement of students. Indeed, research on the referral-to-placement process suggests that teacher decision making is pivotal in determining which students are placed in special education (Anderson, Cronin, and Miller 1986; Artiles and Trent 1994; Gottlieb et al. 1994; McIntyre 1990; Soodak and Podell 1993; Ysseldyke, Christenson, Pianta, and Algozzine 1983). Furthermore, studies suggest that a teacher referral almost invariably leads to special education placement (Algozzine, Christenson, and Ysseldyke 1982). Gartner and Lipsky (1987) report that when some teachers really feel a child needs help, but the test indicates the child is ineligible for special education, a different test is administered in order to increase the chances of a child's eligibility. This is particularly troublesome because teachers have their own biases, prejudices, and racial, ethnic, and social-class stereotypes, which in turn may influence referral decisions (Harry 1992; Ysseldyke and Algozzine 1983).

Links Academic Grouping Has to Discrimination

Academic grouping is contentious not only because of the use of biased standardized tests but also because of its links with discrimination. An abundance of literature has documented that minority students have been (Chinn and Hughes 1987; Deno 1970; Dunn 1968; Eyler, Cook, and Ward 1983; Gartner 1986; Gartner and Lipsky 1987; Heller, Holtzman, and Messick 1982; Hochschild 1984; Mercer 1982; Oakes 1985; Ogbu 1978; Wright and Santa Cruz 1983) and continue to be (Agada and Obiakor 1994; Artiles and Trent 1994; Braddock and Dawkins 1993; Brantlinger 1993; Meier and Stewart 1991; Meier, Stewart, and England 1989, 1991; Polinard, Wrinkle, and Longoria 1990; Schwartz 1990) disproportionately overrepresented in lower-level academic groups, including special education. This overrepresentation remains even when researchers control for student background and past achievement (Braddock and Dawkins 1993; Finley 1984; Lee and Bryk 1988; Oakes 1985; Schafer and Olexa 1971).

American Indians are overrepresented and disproportionately overclassified in low ability tracks, including EMR classes, below basic level classes, and vocational classes (Beare 1986; Braddock and Dawkins 1993; Chinn and Hughes 1987; Dodd and Nelson 1989; Eberhard 1989; Glass 1986; Hillabrant et al. 1992; Indian Nations at Risk Task Force 1991; Latham 1984; Newell and Tyon 1989; O'Brien 1990a; Reyhner 1992a, 1992b; Useem 1990). In many cases, American Indians have the largest percentage of students in these ability tracks.

Some may question whether the disproportionate overrepresentation of minority students in low ability and special education classes is actually a problem. Some previous research argues that this is a problem because it is a way to preserve class and skin color advantages and privileges (Brantlinger 1993; Gartner and Lipsky 1987). It is also a problem because of special educations deleterious effects, as discussed below. The problem of disproportionate placement of minority students in low ability and special education classes has gained such prominence that it has evoked congressional concern about segregation and resegregation and established the need for more compliance reviews by OCR, especially given recent reviews that find many academic grouping practices to be discriminatory (Armstrong 1991; Thompson 1991).

Academic Grouping Conflicts with Integration

Academic grouping is in conflict with school integration. One benefit of integration is that it makes discrimination against minority students more difficult to achieve. Another benefit of integration is that minority students in integrated schools perform higher than in schools that are not integrated. Educating students with disabilities in integrated settings ensures their "normalized community participation" by providing them with systematic instruction in the skills essential to their success in the social, environmental, and political contexts in which they will ultimately use these skills (Gartner and Lipsky 1987). Additionally, teaching students of low or average abilities together with students of higher abilities improves the achievement of the students with lower abilities. The process of school integration requires positive intergroup interaction (Pettigrew 1991, 1994). In the words of Meier, Stewart, and England (1989: 26), "Integration requires equal educational opportunities, equal group status, and cross-racial student contact."

Academic grouping techniques are in direct conflict with the goals of integration. For instance, in some school districts the special education classes are outside the regular school building (Sires and Tonnesen 1993), which results in students being taught in isolation (Gartner and Lipsky 1987; Singer and Bulter 1987; Singer et al. 1986). Gartner and Lipsky (1987: 368) suggest that academic grouping creates separate groups of students with separate programs and even completely separate systems: "The assumptions underlying separate programs have produced a system that is both segregated and second class."

Effectiveness of Academic Grouping

Given the facts that academic grouping (1) involves using racially biased standardized tests (which leads to overrepresentation of minorities in low ability and special education classes) and (2) conflicts with the goals of school integration (equal educational opportunities, equal group status, and cross-racial student contact), such practices seem justifiable only if they enhance the educational achievement of students (Meier, Stewart, and England 1989). Theoretically, under academic grouping, achievement should increase in the following manner. Ability grouping increases student achievement by reducing the disparity in student ability levels, which increases the likelihood that teachers can provide instruction that is neither too easy nor too difficult for most students. The assumption is that ability grouping allows the teacher to increase the pace and raise the level of instruction for high achievers. High achievers benefit from having to compete with one another. Teachers are also able to provide more remedial help, individual attention, repetition, and review for low achievers, who benefit from not having to compete with their more able peers, which may lead to frustration. Low achievers may even be placed into special education classes, in which case the basic premise is that students with deficits will benefit from a unique body of knowledge and from smaller classes staffed by specially trained teachers using special materials. This arrangement is viewed by some as an efficient and effective mechanism to accommodate the differences in student interests and ability.

Research in support of these arguments for academic grouping is not nearly as widely known as research that is critical of ability grouping. However, in several reviews of research on ability grouping Kulik and Kulik (1984, 1987) conclude that accelerated programs confer definite academic benefits for gifted students. Additionally, there is growing research that offers "mixed findings" concerning academic grouping practices. Ability grouping has no impact for average and low ability groups but has benefits for high ability groups (see France-Kaatrude and Smith 1985; Kulik and Kulik 1982; Mills and Durden 1992; Schunk 1987).

Nevertheless, many tend to view the process of grouping very skeptically. For instance, Brantlinger (1993) believes that the sorting of students in schools is integrally political. Ogbu (1986) argues that school socialization is geared toward the development of instrumental competencies required for adult economic and politically structured inequalities. Similarly, Bowles and Gintis (1976) argue that class inequities in education are intentional and result from the deliberate efforts on the part of the power elite to maintain their advantages. Thus, middle-class interests, rather than lower-class inadequacies, are responsible for the persistence of inequalities in educational opportunities and outcomes. Generally, schools, and more specifically teachers, serve as gatekeepers to entrance into power positions, and the sorting of students fits them into a hierarchical socioeconomic class structure (McLaren 1987; Oakes 1988). Standardized tests are often used as a mechanism of social control that gives decision makers, usually teachers, results on which control decisions are based, although even then the members of the advantaged social group will try to advocate treating their failing children in ways that maintain their advantageous status as much as possible (Gartner and Lipsky 1987).

One of the most vocal critics of academic grouping is Robert Slavin. His meta-analysis of numerous studies on ability grouping found that such grouping has no positive effects on academic achievement (Slavin 1987, 1988). This finding is reinforced by other research (see Gamoran 1986, 1992; Mecca 1992; Oakes 1985, 1988). In fact, Mecca (1992) suggests that academic grouping, and more specifically tracking, impairs learning. Additionally, Gamoran (1992) argues that academic grouping and tracking do not increase achievement; rather, they promote inequality. More recently, Slavin and Braddock (1993; and also Braddock and Slavin 1993) reviewed academic grouping and concluded that it is ineffective, harms many, damages interracial relations, and undermines our democratic society and values.

Similarly, special education is also viewed as ineffective. Madden and Slavin's (1982) study of programs for academically handicapped students reports no consistent benefits associated with full-time special education programs. Instead, they find regular class placements to be more beneficial for student achievement, self-esteem, and behavior (Madden and Slavin 1982). A parallel finding is forwarded by Carlberg and Kavale (1980) after reviewing fifty special education studies. Additionally, more recent studies that examine some of the more specific classes of special education find similar conclusions: EMR and LD classes do not show positive effects on students (Artiles and Trent 1994; Gartner and Lipsky 1987; Gottlieb et al. 1994; Mecca 1992; Mercer 1987).

Given the lack of empirical evidence on the benefits of special education, it is not surprising that so-called special education benefits have been described as myths (Gartner 1986; Schwartz 1990). Moreover, special education is not administratively nor instructionally supportable when measured against legal requirements, effective schools research, or fiscal consideration (Bickel and Bickel 1986; Gartner and Lipsky 1987). In sum, it appears that academic grouping is ineffective for students in special education classes and for average and lower than average ability students. Academic grouping may benefit gifted students. However, several other issues also need to be considered. Academic grouping is permanent, often involves misclassification, and creates special education classes that have deleterious effects.

Permanence of Academic Grouping

The decision to group students is crucial because as stated by Meier, Stewart, and England (1989: 25), "Academic grouping creates permanent educational routes for children" (see also Braddock and Dawkins 1993; Levin 1975; Oakes 1985). High ability group placement almost always leads to high aspirations, including college. Conversely, low placement leads to low ambitions with few of these students going to college. Once a student is placed into a low ability group, he or she miss out on experiences and necessary information that severely restricts future opportunities. Students in the lower groups are not taught the same material that is taught in high ability classes. This virtually assures that mobility for students in low ability classes will not be available (see Elder 1983; Mecca 1992; Oakes 1985; Schafer and Olexa 1971).

One reason that special education students do not move from their classes is that they are infrequently reevaluated (Gartner and Lipsky 1987). It seems unconscionable to send a child to special education on a one-way ticket, but as Mecca (1992: 58) eloquently states, "[Systems using academic grouping] often become virtual caste systems, seriously circumscribing the educational opportunities of vast numbers of students."

Classification Problems Are Often Associated with the Use of Academic Grouping

Another problem associated with academic grouping is that minority students, including American Indians, are often misclassified (see Artiles and Trent 1994; *Guadalupe Organization v. Tempe Elementary School District No. 3* 1972; Reschly 1987). Evidence presented in the case of *Hobson v. Hansen* (1967) shows that after reevaluation by school psychologists, two-thirds of the students assigned to the lowest tracts in the District of Columbia schools had been inaccurately evaluated. Elder (1983) finds that half the students in his study would have had different initial group placements if reading readiness had been the only criterion. Ysseldyke and others (1983) conducted a five-year longitudinal study on placement of learning disabled students and found that students are usually tested with inadequate instruments, which leads to "inconsistent and inherently problematic learning disabled definitions and criteria." Other researchers report that at least half of the learning disabled students in public schools could, among other things, be more accurately described as children who are naughty in class (Shepard, Smith, and Vojir 1983). More recently, Gottlieb and others (1994) argue that the bulk of the children labeled learning disabled are not correctly classified (see also Ysseldyke and Algozzine 1983). Smith (1983) reports that the OCR studied 148 school districts between 1975 and 1979 and found that many of the students assigned to EMR classes had never received an examination and that in some cases the assignment was based in part on outdated IQ scores. Many students were assigned to EMR classes even though their IQ test scores were above the EMR range.

Another serious classification issue developing over the last fifteen to twenty years involves the large number of students being labeled as learning disabled. This trend is occurring concomitantly with a decrease in those labeled as mentally retarded (Artiles and Trent 1994; Brantlinger 1993; Cummins 1992; Gartner and Lipsky 1987; Gottlieb et al. 1994; MacMillan 1988; Mercer 1987; Ortiz and Yates 1983). Cummins (1992) argues that litigation and legislation during the 1960s and 1970s, most notably the Education of All Handicapped Children Act of 1975, were designed to address the overrepresentation of minorities in mental retardation classes, such as EMR classes. On the surface, the legislation and litigation seemed to correct the problem. However, recent evidence suggests that the education system started disproportionately placing minorities into classes for the learning disabled in order to reduce their overrepresentation in other areas, like EMR classes (Cummins 1992). Recent studies also show that the pattern of overrepresentation of minorities in EMR and TMR classes still exists (Meier and Stewart 1991; Meier, Stewart, and England 1989; Polinard, Wrinkle, and Longoria 1990), even while minorities are also overrepresented in LD classes (Ortiz and Yates 1983).

American Indians in particular have experienced disproportionately high classifications as LD (Chinn and Hughes 1987; Dodd and Nelson 1989; Hillabrant et al. 1992; Indian Nations at Risk Task Force 1991; Johnson 1992; Latham 1984; O'Connell 1987; Yates 1987); they have more children classified as LD than any other minority group. O'Connell (1987) reports the percentage of American Indian children labeled as LD at 5.28 percent, whereas the percentage is 4.26 percent for African Americans and 4.14 percent for Hispanics and whites. Overrepresentation is likely due to biased standardized tests and classification problems.

Gartner and Lipsky (1987) are more concerned with the accuracy of the learning disabled label than with the excessive number of students classified as learning disabled. They highlight research that discusses major classification problems with the learning disabled label. One study shows that more than 80 percent of the student population can be classified as learning disabled by one or more of the definitions presently used (Shepard, Smith, and Vojir 1983). Another analysis reports that experienced evaluators cannot tell the differences between those already certified as learning disabled and those not, as well as differences between those certified as learning disabled and average learners (Davis and Shepard 1983). Similarly, Shepard (1987: 327) claims that about 90 percent of the children served in special education are mildly handicapped and that these children are virtually "indistinguishable from other low achievers." Not only are children who are classified with learning disabilities indistinguishable from many average and low ability learners; they are also indistinguishable from students classified as educable mentally retarded (Korinek 1987). Gottlieb and others (1994) find that many students with borderline mental retardation are being classified as learning disabled. Generally, however, the special education category that evokes the largest controversy remains mental retardation, especially EMR (see Messick 1984), and not LD.

Deleterious Effects of Academic Grouping and Special Education

Several studies conclude, after controlling for demographic variables, that academic grouping promotes lower self-esteem among students, especially teenagers (Artiles and Trent 1994; Braddock and Slavin 1993; Eyler, Cook, and Ward 1983; Metz 1978; Oakes 1985). Brantlinger (1993) points out that students experience considerable stress about special education placement decisions. This stress is so great in many students that they appear to conceal or repress any memory of their placement. In addition to low self-esteem and other psychological problems, being placed into a low academic group leads to increased frustration, lower expectations, misconduct, delinquency, and school dropout (Artiles and Trent 1994; Braddock and Slavin 1993; Gamoran and Mare 1989; Gartner 1986; Meier, Stewart, and England 1989; Rosenbaum 1976; Schwartz 1990; Slavin 1981, 1988; Slavin and Braddock 1993). Labeling theorists believe that a self-fulfilling prophecy is at work when academic grouping is used. Low ability labeling decreases teacher expectations of students, who in turn have likely already lowered their own aspirations by internalizing their label as a measure of self-worth.

Essentially what occurs with academic grouping, and more specifically being placed into a lower academic group, is a cycle of restricted opportunity that often begins at the early elementary levels and is cumulative (Braddock and Dawkins 1993; Grant and Rothenberg 1986; Mecca 1992; Oakes 1985). For instance, Grant and Rothenberg (1986: 29) state, "For most children in public schools, assignment to an elementary reading group (which usually occurs in first grade) is a critical first step in a sorting process that channels some toward success, some toward moderate levels of achievement, and some toward failure." By the time students reach the secondary level, the inequality of educational opportunities has become more pronounced and problematic. In sum, academic grouping denies many students, including

American Indians, equal educational opportunities and undermines their life chances.

DISCIPLINARY PRACTICES

Disciplinary practices are used to maintain order in schools. Suspensions, which are examined in this research, are used in over 90 percent of public school districts, making them the most widely used type of discipline (Mansfield and Farris 1992). Studies show that ethnic and racial disparities are present among disciplinary practices, including suspensions (Arnez 1978; Brantlinger 1993; Eyler, Cook, and Ward 1983; Jordan, Lava, and McPartland 1994; 1991; McFadden et al. 1992; Meier and Stewart 1991; Meier, Stewart, and England 1989, Wolfgang 1995; Yudof 1975). Although this does not necessarily prove discrimination, it does suggest that the disciplining of American Indian students warrants attention. Schools can use discipline to discourage American Indian students from protesting inequitable conditions and to encourage them to assimilate to white ways. Meier, Stewart, and England (1991) suggest that bureaucratic decision rules in public schools may lead to more punishment of African Americans, since African Americans would be less likely to conform to the values of the white educational system. This seems especially true with regard to American Indians.

Although it is possible that disparities in discipline may not be discriminatory, Meier, Stewart, and England (1989) report that an increasing body of literature supports the conclusion that discipline is used for purposes other than to maintain order (see Froyen 1993; Jordan, Lava, and McPartland 1994; Meier and Stewart 1991; Meier, Stewart, and England 1991; Polinard, Wrinkle, and Longoria 1990). In fact, simply being African American, Hispanic, or American Indian may be an adequate reason for suspension (Arnez 1978; Children's Defense Fund 1974, 1977; Indian Nations at Risk Task Force 1991; McFadden et al. 1992; Reyhner 1992a; U.S. Commission on Civil Rights 1976).

Additionally, discrimination can be a factor in the use of discipline if the disciplinary procedures are not uniformly applied to all students. Put differently, discrimination in discipline can occur in determining what actions are grounds for discipline. Research has shown that minority students, including American Indians, receive more frequent and more severe discipline for infractions similar to those of white students (Balch and Kelly 1974; Brantlinger 1993; Eyler, Cook, and Ward 1983; Marotto 1986; McFadden et al. 1992; Reyhner 1992a; U.S. Commission on Civil Rights 1976). For example, "the average length of suspensions is nearly a day more for minority students than for white students" (HEW as quoted in U.S. Commission on

Civil Rights 1976: 142; see also Arnez 1978; Kaeser 1979).

Research reveals that suspension rates and high dropout rates or low graduation rates go hand in hand (see Arnez 1978; Eyler et al. 1981; Jordan, Lava, and McPartland 1994; Meier and Stewart 1991; Meier, Stewart, and England 1989). Therefore, discipline that is not uniformly applied, especially if it is excessive, can often encourage students to drop out of school, thus reducing educational attainment and contributing to segregation or resegregation (Arnez 1978; Reyher 1992a; Yudof 1975, 1981).

EDUCATIONAL OUTCOMES

Meier, Stewart, and England (1989) suggest that students who endure academic grouping and unequal disciplinary procedures are likely to follow three different courses of action. First, as previously mentioned, the students may drop out of school. Second, the students may attend classes, but not graduate. Finally, students may stay in school and graduate, although they receive a lower quality of education than many white students.

This research analyzes high school graduation rates, which have been used in the past as a measure of educational outcomes (Meier and Stewart 1991; Meier, Stewart, and England 1989, 1991; Polinard, Wrinkle, and Longoria 1990). However, the last course of action that a student may take has received the least amount of attention in the research, although it may be the most important. As previously discussed, academic grouping causes students to receive systematically different experiences, which have a profound affect on their educational attainment. Mecca (1992: 59) states, "Given the sub-par education received by many low-track students one can not help but come to the conclusion that tracking diminishes the educational attainment [or educational quality] of many students." One study analyzing the impact of academic grouping on educational attainment finds that students placed in lower academic groups attain significantly lower grade-point averages, lower rates of academic improvement, and higher rates of dropping out and delinquency than did students in higher academic groups, even when controlling for father's education, IQ, and previous grade-point average (Schafer and Olexa 1971).

The paucity in research analyzing educational quality and second generation discrimination is most likely due to the controversy on how to measure educational quality. In other research, test scores are the typical measures of educational quality. Whether this measure is appropriate is debatable. Student test scores are often not comparable between states because they use different standardized tests.

Over the years many problems have been identified in the education of American Indians. Perhaps the most widely documented and longest recorded problem is the high dropout and low graduation rates (Colodarci 1983; Coombs 1970; Eberhard 1989; Giles 1985; Hill 1993; Indian Nations at Risk Task Force 1991; Latham 1985, 1989; O'Brien 1990a; Pavel et al. 1995; Reyhner 1992a; Swisher 1994a; Swisher and Hoisch 1992; Swisher, Hoisch, and Pavel 1991; Yates 1987). American Indians have the highest high school dropout rate in the nation. Indeed, as many as 35 percent drop out, and in some places, especially urban areas, 50 to 60 percent of American Indian students leave school early, as compared to 22 percent for African Americans, 28 percent for Hispanics, and 15 percent for whites (O'Brien 1990a).

Additionally, American Indians have the lowest educational attainment level of all minority groups. Only 56 percent of the American Indian population twenty-five years or older are high school graduates, compared to 67 percent of the overall population (O'Brien 1990b; Hillabrant et al. 1992; Tippeconnic 1991). Of all minority groups, American Indians have the lowest number of students in college. Only 6.0 percent of the entire Native population, including American Indians, have a college degree. For whites, the comparable statistic is 23 percent (B. Wright 1992). Although high dropout and low graduation rates for American Indians are widely documented, explanations for these educational outcomes for American Indians are relatively unknown (Reyhner 1992a; Swisher and Hoisch 1992). Research suggests for African Americans and Hispanics that high dropout and low graduation rates are associated with second generation discrimination (Meier and Stewart 1991; Meier, Stewart, and England 1989, 1991).

A POLITICAL THEORY OF ACCESS TO EQUAL EDUCATIONAL OPPORTUNITIES

Our research is concerned with the impact of American Indian representation on educational policies that affect American Indian student access to equal educational opportunities. This political theory of access to equal educational opportunities closely follows the logic associated with the theory of representational politics, which includes three models of American Indian representation. Therefore, in addition to American Indian representation, American Indian political resources, social class, and school district size are included in this theory of educational policymaking.

American Indian Teachers

In previous discussions about the discretion of school board members, administrators, and teachers, the hypothesis offered is that the most likely individuals to influence access to equal educational opportunities are teachers. This is expected for several reasons, all of which revolve around the discretion that teachers possess (see Bickel 1982; Cohen 1982; Cummins 1992; Lipsky 1980; McIntyre 1990; Meier and Stewart 1991; Meier, Stewart, and England 1989, 1991; Polinard, Wrinkle, and Longoria 1990; Schwille, Porter, and Gant 1980; Soodak and Podell 1993; Weick 1976; Wirt and Kirst 1989). First, teachers are the implementing-level bureaucrats in a school system; they must actually apply decisions made by administrators and policies passed by the school board. Furthermore, teachers not only implement educational policy but also develop it. Teachers possess considerable discretion that can be used in the process of implementing or making policy decisions.

Teacher expectations, which are related to performance (see Holliday 1985), can influence decisions on ability grouping and tracking. The ethnicity or race of the teachers is associated with their expectations, as well as with how they use their discretion (see Meier and Stewart 1991; Meier, Stewart, and England 1989, 1991; Polinard, Wrinkle, and Longoria 1990). Our research suggests several reasons why the race or ethnicity of the teacher is important. These reasons include the following: Contact and communication between lower-level bureaucrats (teachers) and clients (students) is often facilitated if bureaucrats are representative of the clients (Thompson 1976). There may be greater empathy between co-ethnic teachers and students (Polinard, Wrinkle, and Longoria 1990; Smith and June 1982; So 1987). A representative bureaucracy, in this case among teachers, implies an openness of the government to all individuals, in which case different minority teachers serve as role models to respective minority students (Meier and Stewart 1991; Meier, Stewart, and England 1989). The representativeness of teachers might foster an increased awareness and sensitivity to ethnic and racial issues (Meier, Stewart and England 1989, 1991; U.S. Commission on Civil Rights 1976).

Research dealing specifically with American Indian students shows that in classes with American Indian teachers the students are likely to speak up and participate in class more so than in classes taught with non–American Indian teachers (Reyhner 1992b; Swisher 1990; Swisher and Deyhle 1989; Tonemah 1991). Thus, it is expected that American Indian teachers are more sensitive and receptive to the particular concerns and needs of American Indian students. American Indian teachers serve as role models to American Indian students, thus illustrating the potential of succeeding in the education system and demonstrating to young American Indian students that such aspirations are attainable (Cummins 1992; Indian Nations at Risk Task Force 1991; Noley 1992; Reyhner 1992b; Tonemah 1991).

In sum, American Indian representation should mitigate the amount of second generation discrimination. With their decision-making power and freedom of discretion at the implementing level, teachers are the most likely individuals to affect policy.

American Indian Resources

Meier, Stewart, and England (1989) and Meier and Stewart (1991) argue that minority resources, or in this case American Indian resources, can affect equal educational opportunities in two different ways. First, high levels of American Indian resources indicate that the American Indian community has the potential as a group to pressure the school district for educational policies favorable to American Indian students. Additionally, high levels of American Indian resources also indicate that individual American Indian parents may have the ability to resist a negative decision or policy affecting their children.

Two measures of American Indian political resources are used. The first measure, percentage of American Indians in the district who have graduated from high school, is also used in the representation models. An additional measure is the ratio of American Indian mean family income to white mean family income. This measure is an attempt to assess the level of American Indian resources compared with the level of white resources (see Fraga, Meier, and England 1986; Meier and Stewart 1991; Meier, Stewart, and England 1989; for similar measures using different minority groups).

It is expected that American Indian resources should decrease the amount of second generation discrimination against American Indian students. More specifically, higher levels of American Indian resources should be associated with fewer American Indian students in low academic groups (EMR and LD classes) and proportionately more in high academic groups (gifted classes). American Indian resources should also be related with lower levels of discipline (suspensions) among American Indian students and with more American Indian students graduating.

Social Class

The power theory of intergroup relations that applied to American Indian representation also applies to American Indian student access to equal educational opportunities. The argument is that academic grouping and discipline will have a social-class bias. Second generation discrimination is a function of both race and social class. Lower-class white students will also be adversely affected by academic grouping and disciplinary procedures. Middle-class American Indians should receive better treatment in school districts with more lower-class white students (see Rosenbaum 1976). Furthermore, as Meier, Stewart, and England (1989: 35) note, "The limited size of the lower-ability and special education classes means that fewer 'discretionary' positions will be available for African American students [or American Indian students, in this case]." It is expected that a large white lower class is associated with proportionately more American Indian students in high ability groups and fewer in the low ability groups. Likewise, fewer American Indian students should be disciplined and more should graduate from high school.

School District Size

School district size may affect second generation discrimination. Schools with larger enrollments are more likely to have heterogeneous school populations. This condition may in turn increase demands for minority representation on school boards and in administrative and teaching positions. Viewed in this manner, school district size is expected to decrease second generation discrimination (see Fitzgerald and Morgan 1977; Giles 1975).

Meier, Stewart, and England (1989) and Meier and Stewart (1991) find a negative relationship between school district size and second generation discrimination, however. Their explanation for this finding is that "...larger districts are more likely to be aware of civil rights laws and regulations and are more likely to have had contact with the Office for Civil Rights." An alternative explanation they offer is that large school districts are more likely to have a greater division of labor, which results in greater professionalization. This explanation suggests that school district size may be negatively associated with American Indian levels of second generation discrimination.

CONCLUSION

This chapter provides a justification for a political view of school systems and links school district policies to the political process. Additionally, we introduce our theory of minority representation. This theory has been used to account for African American and Hispanic representation on school boards, in administrative positions, and on teaching faculties (Meier and

Stewart 1991; Meier, Stewart, and England 1989). The chapter shows how this theory is also applicable to American Indian representation and American Indian student access to equal educational opportunities. American Indian representation in policymaking positions is viewed as a function of American Indian political resources, social class, and race. Finally, the theory links representation in policymaking positions to differences in public policy, with policy being a function of American Indian representation, American Indian political resources, race, social class, and school district size.

NOTE

1. The percentage of all residents who are American Indian is used rather than the percentage of the voting-age population. Although this overestimates the number of registered voters, it is consistent with past efforts to explain minority representation (see Dye and Renick 1981; Fraga, Meier, and England 1986; Meier and Stewart 1991; Meier, Stewart, and England 1989).

Chapter 4

Research Design and Measurement of Variables

This chapter is organized into three sections. First, the research design used in the study is discussed. Next, data sources are outlined. Finally, the measurement of dependent and independent variables employed in the research is explained.

RESEARCH DESIGN

Most studies of second generation discrimination either use a quantitative, aggregate approach that involves a large number of school districts (Meier and Stewart 1991; Meier, Stewart, and England 1989; Polinard, Wrinkle, and Longoria 1990) or take the form of qualitative case studies (Metz 1978; Oakes 1985; Rosenbaum 1976; U.S. Commission on Civil Rights 1977). In contrast, this research is designed to benefit from the advantages of each approach—quantitative aggregate analysis and qualitative case study analysis (Goggin 1986; King, Keohane, and Verba 1994). This "holistic approach" to understanding second generation discrimination requires a three-stage research design, the results of which are shown in chapters 5, 6, and 7.

The first stage of the research is summarized in chapter 5. In this part of the analysis the incidence of second generation discrimination is measured using representation ratios, which are described in greater detail below. Using the representation ratios from the first stage of analysis as dependent variables, in chapter 6 we test our theoretical model as outlined in chapter 3. Testing the model requires quantitative analyses at the aggregate level. The purpose of stage two of the analysis is to *explain* the incidence of second generation discrimination. Finally, the third stage of the research design is implemented in chapter 7, which presents our five qualitative case studies. These case studies provide a better understanding of the dynamics of second generation discrimination and suggest strategies for mitigating second generation discrimination.

In sum, the research design involves using aggregate data analysis to identify promising relationships between political variables and second generation discrimination. This analysis is followed by intensive within-case analyses, which are designed to illuminate the interesting quantitative findings and relationships. To perform the aggregate data analysis, several data collections are used. The data are described next.

DATA SETS

The aggregate data analysis is based on U.S. public school districts with a minimum enrollment of 1,000 students and at least a 5.0 percent American Indian enrollment. These criteria yield a sample of 128 school districts. Although the criteria used to select our sample are not exactly the same as the criteria used to study second generation discrimination for African Americans (Meier, Stewart, and England 1989) and Hispanics (Meier and Stewart 1991), comparisons among the studies are still possible for two reasons. First, the criteria of the samples are similar, just not exactly the same. Second, our representation ratios for American Indians are calculated in exactly the same manner as the representation ratios for African Americans (Meier, Stewart, and England, 1989) and Hispanics (Meier and Stewart 1991).

Three separate data sources are used to collect information for our sample of school districts. Measures of academic grouping, discipline, educational attainment, and student enrollment are taken from the OCR, *1992 Elementary and Secondary School Civil Rights Survey*. The Office for Civil Rights does not survey every school district every year, however, their sampling methodology produces survey samples that are projectable to the regional, state, and national level.

Information on American Indian income, education, white poverty, and other similar demographic data are taken from the Bureau of the Census, *1990 Housing and Population Survey*, File ST3F-3. This file contains information for school districts aggregated at the school district level, not at the city level.

In order to collect information regarding American Indian representation on school boards and in administrative and teaching positions, surveys were mailed to the superintendents of each of the 128 previously selected school districts. Then follow-up mailings and telephone calls were employed in an attempt to increase the sample size. These efforts resulted in a final response rate of 97 percent or 124 of the original 128 school districts. A statistical profile of our sample school districts is shown in Table 4.1. The most notable observation about the profile is the wide range of variation across the school districts for the various variables.

Table 4.1
Statistical Profile of School Districts in the Study

Variables	Mean	Standard Deviation	Range Low	Range High
Student Enrollment (Total)	5, 129	6,901	1,000	45,617
Whites (%)	65.5	26.2	1.0	92.8
Am. Indians (%)	21.4	24.4	5.0	98.0
High School Graduates				
Whites (%)	66.5	28.0	1.0	97.0
Am. Indians (%)	20.6	26.0	1.0	99.0
Am. Indian-White Income				
Ratio	0.55	0.22	0.17	1.56
White Poverty (%)	10.3	7.3	0.0	63.1
Am. Indian School Board				
Members (%)	11.4	25.3	0.0	100.0
American Indian				
Administrators (%)	7.4	14.8	0.0	100.0
Am. Indian Teachers (%)	6.1	10.2	0.0	56.0
Am. Indians With High				
School Diploma (%)	19.1	9.1	0.0	72.2
School District				
Revenue Per Pupil	$4,442	$1,381	$2,718	$9,019

MEASUREMENT

Determinants of Second Generation Discrimination

The theoretical model presented in chapter 3 suggests that American Indian representation as school board members, as administrators, and especially as teachers influences second generation discrimination. These representation variables are measured as the percentage of American Indian school board members, the percentage of American Indian administrators, and the percentage of American Indian teachers, respectively, in the school district. The measures hypothesized to affect access to these representation positions are American Indian political resources and social class. Additionally, lower-level positions are expected to be influenced by the upper-level positions. That is, American Indian administrators are predicted to be influenced by American Indian school board members, and American Indian teachers are argued to be affected by American Indian school board members and administrators.

American Indian political resources are really votes or voters, measured as the percentage of the American Indian population in the school district. This measure is used rather than the percentage of the voting-age population. Although this overestimates the number of registered voters, it is consistent with past efforts to explain minority representation in representation positions (see Dye and Renick 1981; Fraga, Meier, and England 1986; Meier and Stewart 1991; Meier, Stewart, and England 1989). The other measure of American Indian political resources is "middle-class status" for American Indians, measured as the percentage of American Indians with high school diplomas. Social class should also affect American Indian representation on school boards and in administrative and teaching positions. The specific measure used is the percentage of the white population with an income below the poverty level.

Our theoretical model (see chapter 3) hypothesizes that American Indian representation affects academic grouping, discipline, and educational attainment—our measures of second generation discrimination. Although it can be argued that representation on the school board and among school administrators might affect polices that involve second generation discrimination, teachers with their direct decision-making and discretionary power at the implementing level are the *most likely* to affect them. The measure of American Indian representation is the percentage of American Indian teachers in the school district.

American Indian resources should decrease second generation discrimination against American Indian students. Two measures of America Indian political resources are used. The first is the percentage of American

Indians in the district who have graduated from high school. The other measure is the ratio of American Indian mean family income to white mean family income. The latter measure is an attempt to assess the level of American Indian resources compared with the level of white resources.

Next, social class should affect second generation discrimination: The power thesis of Giles and Evans (1986) and Feagin (1980) applies to second generation discrimination. Discrimination against American Indian students is a function of both race and social class. The specific measure used is the percentage of the white population with an income below the poverty level.

Finally, school district size is argued to affect second generation discrimination. District size should be negatively associated with levels of second generation discrimination. District size is measured by the total school enrollment. The sample mean, standard deviation, and range of values for the independent variables are shown in Table 4.1.

Second Generation Discrimination

The incidence of second generation discrimination is measured by converting the second generation discrimination indicators (academic grouping: EMR, LD, and gifted classes; discipline: suspensions; and educational attainment: graduations) into "representation ratios." Since the concern is with the disproportionate assignment of American Indian students, the most precise measure is an odds ratio, which provides the relative odds of an American Indian student being assigned or disciplined (see Meier and Stewart 1991; Meier, Stewart, and England 1989). The probability that an American Indian will be assigned to a category is divided by the probability that any student will be so assigned.[1] The representation ratio is equal to one (1.0) if American Indian students are treated the same as all other students. It is less than one (1.0) if American Indian students are less likely to be assigned or disciplined, and it is more than one (1.0) if American Indian students are more likely to be assigned or disciplined. Thus, dependent variables are the five second generation discrimination policy representation ratios: the EMR class ratio, the LD class ratio, the gifted class ratio, the suspension ratio, and the graduation ratio. Table 4.2 provides a brief description of each indicator and the calculation of the policy ratios.

From a theoretical perspective, the ratios are based on the concept of equity. The representation ratios are similar in nature to the ones used in a number of previous studies that assess city council and/or school board minority representational equity (see Engstrom and McDonald 1981; Robinson and Dye 1978; Robinson and England 1981).

Aside from the theoretical perspective, the representation ratios also have

Table 4.2
1992 Second Generation Educational Discrimination Measures

Variables	Variable Description	Variable Calculation
Ability Grouping Indicators (1) Gifted/Talented (GT) Programs Ratio	The proportion of American Indians in GT classes divided by the proportion of all students in GT classes.	Total number of American Indians in GT classes divided by the total number of American Indian students. This quotient is then divided by the quotient of the total number of students in GT classes divided by the total number of students in the school system.
(2) Educable Mentally Retarded (EMR) Programs Ratio	The proportion of American Indians in EMR classes divided by the proportion of all students in EMR classes.	Total number of American Indians in EMR classes divided by the total number of American Indian students. This quotient is then divided by the quotient of the total number of students in EMR classes divided by the total number of students in the school system.
(3) Specific Learning Disabilities (LD) Programs Ratio	The proportion of American Indians in LD classes divided by the proportion of all students in LD classes.	Total number of American Indians in LD classes divided by the total number of American Indian students. This quotient is then divided by the quotient of the total number of students in LD classes divided by the total number of students in the school system.
Discipline Indicator (4) Suspension Ratio	The proportion of American Indians suspended was divided by the proportion of all students that were suspended.	Total number of American Indians suspended divided by the total number of American Indian students. This quotient is then divided by the quotient of the total number of students suspended divided by the total number of students in the school system.
Life Chances or Educational Outcome Indicator (5) High School Graduation Ratio	The proportion of American Indians graduating was divided by the proportion of all those students graduating.	Total number of American Indians graduating divided by the total number of American Indian students. This quotient is then divided by the quotient of the total number of students graduating divided by the total number of students in the school system.

a practical side. The old Emergency School Assistance Act held that more than 20 percent overrepresentation of minority children in EMR classes or in suspensions created a presumption of discrimination (Hochschild 1984: 31). Similarly, at one time the Office for Civil Rights specified that an African American EMR ratio of 1.2 would trigger a program review (Bullock 1976 as cited in Meier, Stewart, and England 1989). Moreover, the representation ratios are accepted as indicators of discrimination for three reasons (Meier, Stewart, and England 1991).

First, these measures often show ethnic and racial disparities that disadvantage minority students. These disparities often exist in EMR, LD, and gifted classes (academic grouping measures) as a result of ethnically and racially biased standardized tests that are used to place students. Second, previous research implies that the quality of education received by students is directly related to the placement of the student. That is, the highest quality education is received in gifted classes, whereas the lowest quality is in special education classes (Gartner and Lipsky 1987; Meier, Stewart, and England 1991; Oakes 1985). Third, the representation ratios are interrelated, which suggests treatment that follows a consistent pattern. Meier, Stewart, and England (1989) find that racial disparities in academic grouping are positively correlated with disparities in discipline and that both are negatively correlated with academic achievement.

One additional point should be made about the representation ratios and the school districts included in this study: *they are representative.* This assertion is illustrated by examining the data in Table 4.3, which is calculated in order to determine if school districts in our sample are representative of all school districts in the United States possessing similar characteristics (at least 1,000 students and 5 percent American Indian enrollment). Representation ratios are calculated for American Indians and whites in school districts in our sample and for all school districts in the United States by using a district sampling weight, which is provided in the OCR data set. The statistics, shown in Table 4.3, reveal that our sample is extremely close to the population with regard to our policy indicators. There are *no significant differences* between the sample means and the population means.

CONCLUSION

This chapter described the research design, data, and dependent and independent variables employed in the study. A three-stage research design is employed which first measures the incidence of second generation discrimination. Next, through quantitative, aggregate analysis an attempt is made to explain second generation discrimination. Finally, qualitative case studies are performed to gain a better understanding of the dynamics of second generation discrimination and to suggest strategies for mitigating second generation discrimination.

Three sets of data are used. One data collection comes from the Office for Civil Rights as part of its *1992 Elementary and Secondary School Civil Rights Survey*. Another data set is the Bureau of the Census, *1990 Housing and Population Survey*. The third data set consists of data obtained from a mail survey sent to each of the school districts in the sample.

Finally, the discussion of measurement identified the determinants of second generation discrimination. These indicators included American Indian political representation, American Indian political resources, social class, and school district size. How we measure second generation discrimination was outlined. The measurement involved transforming second generation discrimination indicators into representation ratios.

Table 4.3
Policy Representation Ratios for American Indians and Whites:
A Comparison of Sample School District Means with Population Means

Policy Ratios	Sample Means	Population Means
EMR Classes		
American Indians	1.33	1.37
Whites	0.85	0.84
LD Classes		
American Indians	1.19	1.20
Whites	0.92	0.91
Gifted Classes		
American Indians	0.60	0.57
Whites	1.49	1.46
Suspensions		
American Indians	1.32	1.35
Whites	0.84	0.83
Graduations		
American Indians	0.89	0.89
Whites	1.07	1.08

Note: Population means include all school districts in the United States.

NOTE

1. Representation ratios calculated in a different manner will also be tested in chapters 5 and 6. For these ratios the probability that an American Indian will be assigned to a category will be divided by the probability that any non-American Indian student will be so assigned.

Chapter 5

The Incidence of Second Generation Discrimination among American Indians

As noted in chapter 4, the incidence of second generation discrimination is measured by converting second generation discrimination indicators into "representation" ratios. This chapter examines these representation ratios. First, the descriptive ratios are presented in order to determine if American Indians are adversely affected by academic grouping and discipline, which in turn affects educational outcomes. Next, the interrelationships among these ratios are analyzed through the use of correlation analysis, factor analysis, and multiple regression.

REPRESENTATION RATIOS FOR AMERICAN INDIANS

The data in Table 5.1 indicate *significant differences between American Indians and whites for every representation ratio.* Generally, the most significant differences are identified in suspensions, gifted, and LD classes, followed by EMR classes and finally graduation rates. More specifically, American Indians are overrepresented in EMR and LD classes, as well as suspensions. Conversely, they are underrepresented in gifted classes and in graduation rates. This follows a pattern consistent with second generation discrimination. Furthermore, the ratios are large enough to merit a more detailed investigation and discussion.

Table 5.1
Policy Representation Ratios for American Indians and Whites

Policy Ratios	American Indians			Whites	
	Mean[1]	Standard Deviation	(N)	Mean	Standard Deviation
EMR	1.33**	1.47	118	0.85	0.34
LD	1.19**	0.61	126	0.92	0.30
Gifted	0.60**	0.56	111	1.49	1.07
Suspension	1.32**	0.91	122	0.84	0.25
Graduation	0.89*	0.67	119	1.07	0.41

1. Means are odds ratios of American Indian students to total student body. When calculated in comparison only to white students, the situation is even worse. The American Indian–White ratios are EMR=2.07, LD=1.38, Gifted=0.47, Suspension=1.59, and Graduation=0.88. The representation ratios for American Indians in comparison to non–American Indians are EMR=1.61, LD=1.39, Gifted=0.52, Suspension=1.51, and Graduation=0.96. T-test is used to determine if American Indian and white means are significantly different.

$*$ $p < .05$
$**$ $p < .01$

Academic Grouping

EMR Classes

Of all special education classifications, EMR most heavily relies on the subjective assessments of teachers, guidance counselors, and school administrators (Bickel 1982). Unlike specific LD classifications, which identify students of normal aptitudes but with specific impediments to learning, EMR is a vaguely defined classification that tends to carry the stigma of intellectual slowness. Not only are EMR assignments based on subjective assessments; they also have fewer restrictions placed on entry and require a lower burden of proof for placement (Artiles and Trent 1994; Meier, Stewart, England 1989). Therefore, it follows that EMR classes have the greatest potential for discrimination, although increasing evidence shows that LD classes may be used to separate minority children from their white counterparts (Artiles and Trent 1994; Brantlinger 1993; Cummins 1992; Gartner and Lipsky 1987; Gottlieb et al. 1994; MacMillan 1988; Mercer 1987; Ortiz and Yates 1983).

The American Indian EMR ratio in Table 5.1 is 1.33, meaning that on average across all school districts in the sample American Indians are overrepresented in EMR classes by 33 percent. This is a statistically significant difference from the white EMR ratio of 0.85. The American Indian EMR ratio ranged from a low of 0.00 to a high of 12.70 (a shocking 1170 percent overrepresentation). Thus, in many districts the EMR policy ratio exceeded the mean. For comparison purposes, the average American Indian EMR ratio is significantly lower than the EMR ratio for African Americans (Meier, Stewart, and England 1989: 82), which was 1.95 in the most recent year analyzed. However, the American Indian EMR ratio is substantially higher than the EMR ratio reported for Hispanics (Meier and Stewart 1991: 128), which was 1.13 for the most recent year examined.

LD Classes

Classes for the specific learning disabled require a more precise diagnosis than do EMR classes (e.g., placement for motor skill development, for dyslexia, for speech therapy or for occupational therapy). Thus, the burden of proof is greater and often involves outside actors such as medical doctors and educational consultant or advocates. Thus, discriminatory LD placement is more difficult, although it can still occur (see Ortiz and Yates 1983; Tucker 1980).

Table 5.1 reveals overrepresentation of American Indians in LD classes by 19 percent. Although overrepresentation ratio is smaller than the EMR ratio, the ratio is significantly different from the white LD ratio, which is 0.92. For comparative purposes, Meier and associates (see Meier and Stewart 1991: 163) report relative racial equity for LD representation ratios. For African American students the LD ratio is 1.04, and for Hispanic students, 0.96. The American Indian LD ratio ranged from a low of 0.00 to a high of 4.62.

Gifted Classes

Gifted classes are generally seen as the best education that a school district offers (Eyler, Cook, and Ward 1983; Gartner and Lipsky 1987; Meier, Stewart, and England 1991; Oakes 1985). These classes normally represent the highest quality of education that students can receive from a school district and often result in intense competition for limited spaces. Access to gifted classes provides students with a solid educational base for college by exposing them to the best teachers the school district has to offer and to the most challenging classes (Gartner and Lipsky 1987; Mecca 1992).

According to Table 5.1, American Indians have much lower chances of placements in gifted classes than do white students. The gifted ratio is 0.60, which means that American Indians are underrepresented in gifted classes by 40 percent. In contrast, whites are about 2.5 times more likely than American Indians to be enrolled in gifted classes—a difference that is statistically significant. Additionally, analysis of the variation in the American Indian gifted ratio finds that approximately 60 percent of the school districts are below the mean. Still, it is encouraging to note that American Indian gifted ratios are higher, although only marginally, than those reported for African Americans, 0.45 in 1984 (Meier, Stewart, and England 1989: 82) and Hispanics, 0.52 in 1986 (Meier and Stewart 1991: 130).

Discipline

Suspensions

Meier and Stewart (1991) report that suspensions affect over 6 percent of the student population annually and are twice as frequent as corporal punishment. As a result, suspensions may have a major influence on a student's access to education. Table 5.1 shows that American Indians are disproportionately suspended: They are 32 percent more likely to be suspended than the average student. Conversely, whites are about 15 percent less likely to be suspended than the average student. These differences are statistically significant. The range for the American Indian suspension ratio is from a low of 0.00 to a high of 5.88. Similar to the pattern identified for EMR ratios, the American Indian suspension ratio is considerably lower than that of African Americans, 1.59 in 1984 (Meier, Stewart, and England 1989: 85). However, this ratio is far above the suspension ratio for Hispanics, 1.10 in 1986 (Meier and Stewart 1991: 133).

Educational Outcome

Graduation Rates

Previous literature on second generation discrimination has shown that ethnic and racial disparities can adversely affect graduation rates. Although graduation rates are influenced by numerous factors beyond the educational system and school teachers or administrators, the graduation rate is used as an indirect measure of educational quality or educational equity. In Table 5.1 we see that the American Indian graduation rate is lower than the graduation rate for whites. Based on their student numbers, American Indians graduate at about 10 percent below the rate expected. However, given the amount of literature devoted to the issue, it is somewhat surprising that the American Indian graduation ratio is not even lower . The graduation ratio for American Indians is equal to the one reported for African Americans, 0.89 in 1984 (Meier, Stewart, and England 1989: 87), and is somewhat higher than the ratio reported for Hispanics, 0.78 in 1986 (Meier and Stewart 1991: 135). Nevertheless, the difference between graduation rates, on average, for American Indian students and white students is statistically significant.

SUMMARY OF REPRESENTATION RATIOS

To this point we have identified overrepresentation of American Indians for policy ratios that negatively affect American Indian students (EMR and LD classes and suspensions) and underrepresentation for measures that have positive effects on students (gifted classes and graduation rates). The situation for American Indians is even worse when the representation ratios are calculated in comparison only to white students or only non-American Indians (see footnote in Table 5.1). The pattern in representation ratios we report here for American Indians is very similar to the pattern for African Americans and Hispanics and supports the theory of second generation discrimination. Additional research to examine the interrelationships of the second generation discrimination indicators—representation ratios—is needed to further test this theory.

ANALYSIS OF THE INTERRELATIONSHIPS OF SECOND GENERATION DISCRIMINATION

Intercorrelations

Meier, Stewart, and England (1989) argue that if representation ratios reflect nothing more than good educational practices, then many of the policies should be unrelated to each other. That is, there is no apparent reason why the placement of American Indian students in EMR or LD classes should be related to the suspension of American Indian students. Similarly, the number of American Indian students suspended should be unrelated to the placement of American Indian students in gifted classes. However, if the ratios reflect some measure of ethnic, racial, or class discrimination, a predictable pattern of intercorrelations should exist. The pattern is such that all indicators that reflect positively on the student (gifted classes and graduation rates) should be positively related to each other. Additionally, all of the indicators that reflect negatively on students (EMR, LD, and suspension rates) should be positively related to each other. Finally, correlations between positive actions and negative actions (i.e., gifted classes and suspensions) should be negative.

Table 5.2 presents the intercorrelations for the policy ratios. Eight of the ten correlations are consistent with a hypothesis of discrimination; that is, the correlations are in the predicted direction. The two correlations that do

Table 5.2
Intercorrelations of Policy Representation Ratios

	EMR	LD	Gifted	Suspension	Graduation
EMR	—				
LD	.02	—			
Gifted	-.09	-.21*	—		
Suspension	.37**	.25**	-.34**	—	
Graduation	.04	-.17	.06	.06	—

*   p<.05
** p<.01

not follow the discrimination pattern involve graduation rates. The correlation between EMR and graduation is positive and the correlation between suspension and graduation is positive when both are hypothesized to be negative. As noted above, graduation rates are more likely than the other measures to be affected by a number of factors exogenous to the school system. Furthermore, the two correlations in the wrong direction are not statistically significant. Conversely, of the eight correlations following the second discrimination hypothesis, four are statistically significant. Moreover, the strong correlations between all three academic groups (EMR, LD, and gifted) and suspensions is difficult to explain without a reference to racial discrimination. As past research argues (Meier and Stewart 1991: 141), "If an EMR placement helps a student, then the student should learn more [and be less frustrated] and be less likely to be a disciplinary problem." Comparatively, the correlation between American Indian EMR ratios and suspensions (0.37) is almost identical to the one for African Americans (0.38) and Hispanics (0.36), providing more support for the second generation discrimination hypothesis. Factor analysis can offer a more detailed method of analyzing the interrelationships among the policy indicators.

Factor Analysis

Previous research examining second generation discrimination uses factor analysis to determine the presence of a "clustering" of the policy ratios; that is, whether there is a common core among the measures that can actually be termed second generation discrimination (for African Americans see Meier, Stewart, and England 1989; Wainscott and Woodard 1988; for Hispanics see Meier and Stewart 1991). The argument is similar to the one made for the correlation analysis. Since second generation discrimination is a "negative" process (i.e., represents discrimination), the second generation discrimination hypothesis predicts actions that have positive influences on American Indian students (gifted classes and graduation) should load negatively on a factor, while actions that have negative influences (EMR and LD classes and also suspensions) should load positively on the factor. Put differently, actions that affect American Indians in positive and negative manners will load in opposite directions.

Table 5.3 shows that the five representation policy indicators load on the first factor *exactly as expected.* High school graduates and gifted classes both load negatively, whereas EMR classes, LD classes, and suspensions load positively. This is also consistent with the predicted and determined clustering for the correlations. Moreover, the strongest factor loadings form two strong associations. First, large suspension loadings are associated with a lack of gifted class placement. Furthermore, large suspension loadings are associated with a great deal of EMR placement. In general, findings suggest that American Indian overrepresentation in some categories (EMR, LD, and suspensions) and white overrepresentation in others (gifted classes and graduations) can be viewed as two sides of the same conceptual coin.

The single dimension emerging from the factor analysis explains 35 percent of the common variance among the variables and is the same amount found

Table 5.3
Factor Analysis of Policy Representation Ratios

Variables	Factor Loading
EMR Classes	.66
LD Classes	.47
Gifted Classes	-.66
Suspensions	.81
Graduations	-.20
Eigen Value	1.74
Percentage of Variance Explained	35.00

in the single dimension for African Americans in 1984 (Meier, Stewart, and England 1989: 91), although Wainscott and Woodard (1988) argue for two dimensions of second generation discrimination. Interestingly, in the study of Hispanics, Meier and Stewart (1991) find two dimensions of second generation discrimination, although neither factor explained more of the variance than the single dimension found for American Indians or African Americans.

The results from the intercorrelation analysis and the factor analysis establish a pattern of treatment for American Indians that corresponds to our second generation discrimination hypothesis and is comparable to that reported for African Americans (Meier, Stewart, and England 1989), although possibly not as severe or as consistent. The pattern appears to be worse and more consistent than the one reported for Hispanics (Meier and Stewart 1991). To further examine the interrelationships of second generation discrimination, multiple regression is employed.

Multiple Regression

Before discussing findings from the regression analysis, we must consider the theoretical model of the interrelationships of the second generation discrimination measures shown in Figure 5.1. The purpose of the regression analysis is not to fully explain American Indian gifted class enrollments, suspensions, or graduations. Likewise, the argument is not that the underrepresentation of American Indians in gifted classes is determined only by the placement of American Indians in EMR or LD classes. The purpose is to analyze relationships that may exist if second generation discrimination against American Indian students is occurring.

Gifted Classes

According to Meier, Stewart, and England (1989) assignments to gifted classes should not be related to EMR or LD assignments. Theoretically, each type of class should provide educational services for completely different types of students. Nevertheless, the second generation discrimination model holds that academic grouping is a discriminatory process and suggests that school districts with high American Indian EMR and LD ratios will have low American Indian gifted class ratios.

Multiple regression analysis is performed in order to determine if the American Indian gifted assignment ratio is a function of EMR or LD classes[1] (see Table 5.4). A strong negative relationship exists between assignment ratios for LD classes and gifted assignment ratios. A 1.0 percent increase in the American Indian LD ratio is associated with a 0.39 percent drop in

Figure 5.1
The Interrelationships of Second Generation Educational
Discrimination Measures: Preliminary Model

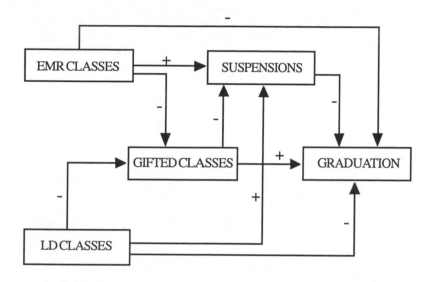

the American Indian gifted class ratio. Additionally, there is a marginally significant relationship between American Indian EMR ratios and the gifted class ratio. A 1.0 percent increase in the American Indian EMR ratio is associated with a 0.19 percent decrease in the American Indian gifted class ratio. The relationship between the EMR class ratio and the gifted class ratio for American Indians is significantly lower than that found in research on African Americans (-0.86 in 1984). However, the impact for American Indians is slightly higher than for Hispanics (-0.17 in 1986).

Suspensions
Figure 5.1 predicts that suspensions are a function of the three academic grouping categories: EMR, LD, and gifted class assignment ratios. Table 5.5 confirms, for the most part, this prediction; LD class ratios are not statistically significant and are deleted from the reduced model. A 1 percent increase in the American Indian EMR class ratio produces a 0.39 percent increase in the suspension ratio, whereas a 1 percent increase in the American Indian gifted class ratio corresponds with a 0.23 percent decrease in the American Indian suspension ratio. The impact of the EMR class ratio on suspensions for American Indians is higher than that for African Americans,

Table 5.4
Gifted Class Assignments as a Function of EMR and LD Class Assignments

Dependent Variable: American Indian Gifted Class Ratio

Independent Variables	Unstandardized Regression Coefficients	Standard Errors
EMR Class Ratio	- 0.19#	0.11
LD Class Ratio	- 0.39**	0.15
Constant	- 0.32	0.03

R^2	=	.10
Adjusted R2	=	.08
F	=	5.08**

\# $p<.10$
** $p<.01$

0.23 in 1984 (Meier, Stewart, and England 1989), and is virtually equal to the impact for Hispanics, 0.40 in 1986 (Meier and Stewart 1991). Additionally, the influence of the gifted class ratios on suspensions with respect to American Indians is substantially greater than the influence of the African American gifted class ratio on African American suspensions, 0.01 in 1984 (Meier, Stewart, and England 1989). A similar relationship is not reported for Hispanics by Meier and Stewart in 1991. In general, the results in Table 5.5 suggest that academic grouping is important in understanding the suspension process, especially for American Indians. Moreover, when compared to other minority groups, the impact may be even greater.

Graduation Rates
The second generation discrimination model culminates with graduation rates, which are used to measure educational attainment. An important point offered by Meier and Stewart (1991) and Meier, Stewart, and England (1989) in earlier studies on second generation discrimination is that denying African Americans or Hispanics equal access to quality education can occur without affecting their graduation rates. That is, the quality of education an African American or a Hispanic graduate receives can be considerably lower than the quality of education a white graduate receives. This is certainly applicable to American Indians.

Table 5.5
Suspensions as a Function of EMR, Gifted, and LD Class Assignments

Dependent Variable: American Indian Suspension Ratio

Independent Variables	Full Model		Reduced Model	
	Unstandardized Regression Coefficients	Standard Errors	Unstandardized Regression Coefficients	Standard Errors
EMR Class Ratio	0.38**	0.08	0.39**	0.08
Gifted Class Ratio	- 0.21**	0.07	- 0.23**	0.07
LD Class Ratio	0.13	0.10		
Constant	- 0.04	0.03	-0.04	0.03
R^2 =		.36		.35
Adjusted R^2 =		.34		.33
F =		15.18**		21.72**

** $p < .01$

According to the second generation discrimination theory, the American Indian high school graduation ratio should be negatively related to American Indian EMR and LD class ratios and to the American Indian suspension ratio. The American Indian graduation ratio should also be positively associated with the American Indian gifted class ratio. All these relationships, examined in Table 5.6, are found to be in the expected direction. However, only the American Indian gifted class ratio, which is positively related to the American Indian graduation ratio, is statistically significant. Although the impact of this relationship is modest, a 1.0 percent increase in American Indian gifted class ratio translates into a 0.17 percent increase in the American Indian graduation ratio, the impact of the gifted class ratio (0.17 in the reduced model in Table 5.6) is substantially larger than the impact of the African American gifted class ratio on the African American graduation ratio, which is only 0.08 in 1984 (Meier, Stewart, and England 1989: 117). The impact of the gifted class ratio for American Indians is similar to the impact of the gifted class ratio found for Hispanics (Meier and Stewart 1991: 176).

    The results of the multiple regression analysis of the interrelationships between the second generation discrimination indicators provide a much simpler model than the one presented in Figure 5.1. Figure 5.2 displays only the interrelationships between the second generation discrimination measures

Table 5.6
**The Impact of EMR, LD, and Gifted Class Assignments
and also Suspensions on American Indian High School Graduates**

Dependent Variable: American Indian Graduates Ratio

Independent Variables	Full Model		Reduced Model	
	Unstandardized Regression Coefficients	Standard Errors	Unstandardized Regression Coefficients	Standard Errors
Gifted Class Ratio	0.20*	0.10	0.17*	0.08
EMR Class Ratio	-0.01	0.12		
LD Class Ratio	-0.10	0.13		
Suspension Ratio	-0.03	0.15		
Constant	-0.05	0.04	-0.07	0.03
R^2 =		.08		.05
Adjusted R^2 =		.04		.04
F =		1.62		5.01*

* $p<.05$

that are statistically significant. We think it is worth noting that the direction of every relationship in the reduced model (Figure 5.2) follows the second generation discrimination hypothesis as presented in Figure 5.1.

CONCLUSION

This chapter demonstrates that American Indians are significantly overrepresented in policy representation ratios—measures of second generation discrimination—that negatively affect students, namely, EMR classes, LD classes, and suspensions. Conversely, American Indians are substantially underrepresented in representation policy ratios that positively affect students, namely, gifted classes and graduations. Furthermore, we found that the measures of second generation discrimination for American Indians converged or clustered together, whether analyzed through intercorrelation or factor analysis. Multiple regression analysis reveals interrelationships among all the American Indian second generation discrimination indicators. Moreover, analyses of policy ratio means, the intercorrelation analysis, the factor analysis, and the multiple regression analysis establish a pattern of treatment for American Indians that supports

Figure 5.2
The Interrelationships of Second Generation Educational
Discrimination Measures: Final Model

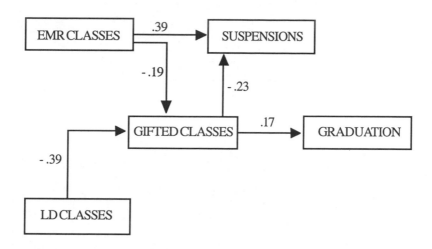

Note: The numbers are the unstandardized regression coefficients.

the second generation discrimination hypothesis. Comparisons to the second generation discrimination study of African Americans identified a similar pattern, although not as severe. However, the second generation discrimination pattern identified for American Indians appears to be worse and more consistent than the one previous research reports for Hispanics.

The intent of this chapter is to suggest that some academic grouping and discipline is attributable to discrimination. This does not mean that all academic grouping and discipline is intentionally discriminatory or "bad." Additionally, this does not mean that other factors such as social class, intelligence, and behavior do not affect academic grouping and discipline decisions. However, it seems likely that an element of second generation discrimination exists for American Indians, as reflected in the measures of academic grouping and discipline. Clearly, a systematic pattern of educational policies with damaging effects on American Indian students, a pattern that is consistent with the theory of second generation discrimination, has been identified. The next chapter attempts to explain the causes of second generation discrimination.

NOTE

1. To avoid problems with extreme cases in the regression analysis, each second generation discrimination measure was subjected to a log transformation (see Tufte 1974).

Chapter 6

Representation in Educational Policymaking: The Impact of American Indian Representation on Second Generation Discrimination

Chapter 5 reveals that American Indians are significantly overrepresented in policy representation ratios that negatively affect students and are significantly underrepresented in areas that positively affect students. This chapter examines American Indian representation in educational policymaking in an effort to determine the impact of representation on the policy ratios analyzed in the last chapter.

Representation is an issue that has captivated the interest of political scientists for centuries. Perhaps the most notable theoretical study of representation is the work of Pitkin (1967), which has been used by many scholars as a cornerstone for their own research. For instance, Mosher (1982), drawing on Pitkin's (1967) descriptive and active views of representation, defines two types of bureaucratic representation: passive representation and active representation. A bureaucracy is representative in the passive sense if bureaucrats share the same demographic origins (ethnicity, race, gender, religion, education, etc.) as the general population. A bureaucracy is perceived as less of a threat to democracy if the bureaucracy is representative of all interests in society (Mosher 1982; Redford 1969). The bureaucracy is seen as less threatening if it mirrors the social origins of the population because it shares the socialization experiences, has similar attitudes, and makes policy decisions similar to those that the populace would make if all citizens participated in all decisions. These arguments and ideas are advanced by advocates of representative bureaucracy, a theory developed, advanced, and/or analyzed by Kingsley (1944), Levitan (1946), Long (1952), Mosher (1968), Meier (1975), and

Saltzstein (1979).

In much of the research focusing on passive representation, comparisons are made at the collective level, between an entire set of representatives and all citizens rather than directly between individual representatives and their constituents (Weisberg 1978). An example of such a comparison could be between the percentage of American Indian representatives on a school board and the percentage of American Indian voters in the population.

On the other hand, according to Mosher (1982), active representation moves beyond passive representation in the sense that a bureaucracy is an active representative if it produces policy outputs that benefit individuals who are passively represented. Similarly, Eulau and Karps (1977) extend Pitkin's (1967) active view of representation with their discussion of policy congruence. They argue that a representative can act in the interests of the represented by having policy congruence—making decisions that are consistent with the policy preferences of the represented. Both of these ideas are based on Pitkin's (1967) idea of active representation, which involves the representative actually doing something.

Although research on passive representation, especially in democratic societies, is certainly justifiable based on the principles of equity and equal access (a patronage view of representation), few scholars have attempted to link passive representation in bureaucracies with active representation by the bureaucrats (but see Meier 1993; Meier and Stewart 1991; Meier, Stewart, and England 1989; Saltzstein 1979, 1983; Thompson 1976, 1978). Meier (1993) concludes that the literature regarding representative bureaucracy for minority groups is missing empirical studies that relate passive representation with active representation. Put differently, we know much about passive representation, but we do not know if passive representation matters; whether it makes a difference in terms of policy outputs.

Linking passive representation with active representation involves determining to what extent passive representation translates into active representation, or discovering whether passive representation produces benefits for those passively represented. More specific to this analysis, the empirical question is whether American Indian representation on school boards and in administrative and teacher positions leads to equal educational opportunities for American Indian students?

As discussed earlier, previous literature suggests that three conditions need to exist in order for passive representation to be linked to active representation (see Meier 1993; Meier and Nigro 1976; Meier and Stewart 1991; Meier, Stewart, and England 1989; Saltzstein 1979, 1983; Thompson

1976, 1978). First, the descriptive characteristic in question must be salient, such as ethnicity or race. Second, individual bureaucrats need to have discretion to act. Finally, policy decisions made by the bureaucracy must be directly relevant to the salient descriptive characteristic of the passively represented. In this case, school district policy decisions regarding American Indian students must be relevant to American Indians in the community.

This chapter examines the impact of American Indian representation on school district policies. First, we examine the descriptive representativeness (the passive representativeness) of three groups—school board members, administrators, and teachers. This analysis includes measuring the levels of American Indian representation and then determining how American Indian representation is gained. Next, the chapter analyzes the linkage between passive and active representation. This analysis seeks to determine whether the representation of American Indians among teachers affects the access of American Indian students to equal educational opportunities. During this stage of the analysis, the measures of second generation discrimination are investigated using our political theory of educational policy, which hypothesizes that American Indian representation, American Indian resources, white poverty, and district size are linked to American Indian second generation discrimination measures.

PASSIVE REPRESENTATION

Levels of American Indian Representation

In comparison to the abundance of literature examining passive minority representation for African Americans and Hispanics, the representation literature on American Indians is virtually nonexistent. Of the small group of studies on American Indian representation, most stress a representative bureaucracy argument, sometimes also called a patronage argument. The representative bureaucracy argument holds that American Indians, for instance, should have the same proportion of positions on a school board or in administrative and teaching faculties as their proportion of the school district population or proportion of American Indian students in the school district (see Barlow 1984; Indian Nations at Risk Task Force 1991; Jones and Montenegro 1982; Lutz and Barlow 1980, 1981; Lynch and Charleston 1990; Noley 1992; Tippeconnic 1991). Thus, if American Indians constitute 20 percent of the total school district enrollment, 20 percent of the teachers in the school district should be American Indians. Such a proportion is viewed as consistent with the values of fairness and equity (see Dye and Renick 1981; Mladenka 1989a) and is easily translated into a representation equity index by dividing the two percentages. When American Indians have political representation exactly equal to their population, the index equals one. However, when American Indians are underrepresented, the index is less than one and the ratio specifies the exact percentage of underrepresentation. Conversely, when American Indians are overrepresented, the index is greater than one and the ratio shows the precise percentage of overrepresentation. A precautionary note regarding the index is warranted. When the percentage of American Indian population is small, any representation at all results in extremely large numbers that distort the index. Nevertheless, use of the index is popular because of its ease in interpretation.

Levels of American Indian Representation on School Boards

The data in Table 6.1 present American Indian representation ratios for school board members, administrators, and teachers. Two points of information about the data in the table are required. First, not all school districts provide complete data about the number of school board members, administrators, and teachers in the district. Thus, the total number of school districts (shown in the last column in Table 6.1) differs among the three

Table 6.1
Representation Ratios for American Indian School Board Members, Administrators, and Teachers

	Mean	Standard Deviation	Number of School Districts
School Board Members[1]	0.46	0.98	78
School Board Members[2]	0.36	0.73	78
Administrators[1]	0.62	1.48	120
Administrators[2]	0.29	0.39	120
Teachers[1]	0.50	0.73	124
Teachers[2]	0.27	0.34	124

1. Using the American Indian population in the school district as the comparison base.
2. Using American Indian student enrollment as the comparison base.

groups of school representatives. Second, for each group of school officials, we offer two representation ratios. The first ratio is calculated using the American Indian population in the school district as the comparison base.

The second ratio uses American Indian student enrollment in the school district as the comparison base. Using the latter comparison base (American Indian student enrollment) significantly lowers the representation index for each group of school representatives. Clearly, one can make a strong argument that American Indian school board members, American Indian administrators, and American Indian teachers should be represented in proportion to the number of their constituents in the *school system* rather than in proportion to the American Indians in the general population. Following the lead of Meier, Stewart, and England (1989), we offer both representation ratios. The more conservative test of underrepresentation is based on American Indian population in the school district as the comparison base. Although others might disagree, we believe that for administrative and teaching positions, the most appropriate comparison base is the number of American Indians in the school enrollment. For school board membership, we believe the American Indian general population is the more appropriate comparison base. Regardless of our normative thoughts, we offer both representation ratios.

With respect to school board members, American Indians occupy 11.49 percent of the total number of school board members in the seventy-eight school districts reporting data. Using our theory of representativeness, American Indians hold only 46 percent of the total number of school board seats they should hold based on their population in the school districts. Using American Indian school enrollment as the comparison base, American Indian school board representation drops to 36 percent of the total number of seats American Indians should occupy based on the theory of representativeness.

Levels of American Indian Representation among Administrators

American Indians hold 7.46 percent of all administrative positions in the school districts in the sample. This translates into a administrator representation index of 0.62. In other words, across the 120 school districts that report data, American Indians hold only 62 percent of the administrative positions they should hold based on the number of American Indians in the school districts. The American Indian representation ratio for administrators using American Indian enrollment as the comparison base is much lower, 29 percent. Using this standard, on average, American Indian administrators are underrepresented in the school districts by 71 percent. For comparison purposes, using African American and Hispanics students as the comparison base, the administrator representation ratio for African Americans is 73 percent (Meier, Stewart, and England 1989: 72) and is 39 percent for Hispanics (Meier and Stewart 1991: 104).

Levels of American Indian Representation among Teachers

American Indians are also underrepresented in teaching positions. American Indians make up 6.10 percent of the overall teaching faculty in the 124 school districts reporting data. The representation ratio for American Indian teachers shows an underrepresentation of 50 percent when American Indian population is used as the comparison base and 73 percent underrepresentation when American Indian school enrollment is used as the comparison base. The American Indian representation ratio for teachers, using American Indian student enrollment as the comparison base, is 37 percent less than that for African American teachers (0.64 representation ratio; Meier, Stewart, and England 1989: 74) and is 11 percent less than that of Hispanic teachers (0.38 representation ratio; Meier and Stewart 1991: 106). Table 6.2 shows that statistically significant differences exist between the mean representation ratio for American Indian and white teachers. This finding is true regardless of which comparison base (population or student enrollment) is used. Indeed, the white teacher representation mean ratio shows significant overrepresentation. The representation ratio ranges from 98 percent using the white population criterion to 233 percent using the white student enrollment criterion.

DETERMINANTS OF AMERICAN INDIAN REPRESENTATION

The data in Tables 6.1 and 6.2 illustrate the underrepresentation of American Indians on school boards and in administrative and teacher positions. In this section of the chapter we examine the determinants of American Indian representation on school boards and in administrative and teaching positions.

American Indian Representation on School Boards

In chapter 3 we argue that American Indian school board representation is influenced by white poverty (percentage of white families in the district below the poverty level) and American Indian resources—American Indian

Table 6.2

Representation Ratios for American Indian and White Teachers

	American Indians			Whites	
	Mean[1]	Standard Deviation	(N)	Mean	Standard Deviation
Teachers[2]	0.50**	0.73	124	1.98	3.21
Teachers[3]	0.27**	0.34	124	3.33	9.58

1. T-test is used to determine if American Indians and whites means are significantly different.

2. Using the American Indian population in the school district as the comparison base for the American Indian representation ratio. Using the white population in the school district as the comparison base for the white representation ratio.

3. Using American Indian student enrollment as the comparison base for the American Indian representation ratio. Using the white student enrollment as the comparison base for the white representation ratio.

** $p<.01$

population (percentage in the school district) and education (percentage of American Indians in school district with high school diplomas). White poverty is the indicator used for the power thesis of intergroup relations, which argues that whites with upper- and middle-level incomes seek to distance themselves from poor whites (Feagin 1980; Giles and Evans 1985, 1986). American Indian resources are needed for political mobilization (Deloria and Lytle 1983; McCool 1985; McDonald 1989; Tippeconnic 1991).

Table 6.3 shows the impact of the three variables on American Indian school board representation. Although the percentage of whites living in poverty does not significantly influence American Indian school board representation, the direction of the effect is positive.

American Indian resources display a mixed picture. American Indian education has no significant effect on school board representation, whereas American Indian population has a strong statistically significant impact. Indeed, for a 1 percent increase in the American Indian population, there is almost a 1 percent increase in American Indian representation on school boards. This strong positive relationship between American Indians in the

Table 6.3
Determinants of American Indian Representation on School Boards (N=73)

Dependent Variable: Percentage of American Indian School Board Members

Independent Variables	Full Model		Reduced Model	
	Unstandardized Regression Coefficients	Standard Errors	Unstandardized Regression Coefficients	Standard Errors
American Indian Population	1.03**	0.05	1.02**	0.05
American Indian Education	0.08	0.11		
White Poverty	0.10	0.23		
Constant	-7.19	3.45	-4.52	1.30
R^2	.87			.87
Adjusted R^2	.86			.86
F	158.78**			483.80**

** $p<.01$

population and American Indian representation on school boards remains even when American Indian education and white poverty are dropped from the regression equation. American Indian population alone explains 86 percent of the variation in American Indian school board representation.

American Indian Representation among School Administrators

An abundance of literature has established that elected officials exercise discretion in policymaking (see Anderson 1984; Eulau et al. 1959; Mladenka 1980; Moe 1982; Prewitt 1970; Rourke 1984). A growing body of literature becoming more widely accepted and recognized presents similar findings for administrators: Administrators possess discretion similar to that of elected officials (Bullock and Lamb 1984; Downs 1967; Lowi 1969; Meier 1987; Meier and Stewart 1991; Meier, Stewart, and England 1989; Rourke 1984).

Because bureaucratic discretion exists, the representativeness of educational bureaucracies (administrators) becomes an important political question for at least two reasons. First, in education policy, not unlike most policy areas in the modern bureaucratic state, problems are often perceived as best left up to the experts (administrators), who can apply their bureaucratic expertise to solve them (Spring 1993; Tyack 1974; Wirt and Kirst 1989; also see Chubb and Moe 1990 for a critique of this practice). Additionally, education is a policy area where reforms have been made in an attempt to insulate decisions from electoral politics (see Chubb and Moe 1990; Spring 1993; Wirt and Kirst 1989). Consequently, administrators have generally been successful in developing a system of decision making that exists within their own professional prerogative (Burlingame 1986; Chubb and Moe 1990; Crowson and Morris 1985; Spring 1993; Wirt and Kirst 1989; Tucker and Zeigler 1980).

According to the theory outlined in chapter 3, American Indian access to administrative positions generally follows a pattern similar to American Indian access to school board seats, except for a few slight changes. The percentage of American Indian administrators in the school district should be a function of American Indian resources (population and education) and white poverty. Additionally, the percentage of American Indian school board members is included. As Table 6.4 shows, the model of bureaucratic representation predicts reasonably well for American Indian school administrators, accounting for slightly over three-fifths of the variance. The regression coefficients reveal that American Indians attain 27 percent of the representation among school district administrators that is expected given their share of population. A 1 percent increase in American Indian population is associated with a 0.27 percent increase in American Indian administrators.

American Indian representation on the school board also has a modest significant impact on administrative representation. A 1.0 percentile increase in American Indian representation corresponds to a 0.21 percentile increase in the representation of American Indian administrators. Another way to express this political linkage is that the addition of one American Indian representative to a five-person school board translates into a 4.2 percentage point increase in American Indian administrators, all other things being equal.

For comparison purposes, the impact of a 1.0 percentile increase in Hispanic school board representation is a 0.16 percentage point increase in the representation of Hispanic administrators. On a five-person school board, one additional Hispanic representative translates into a 3.2 percentage point increase in Hispanic administrators (Meier and Stewart 1991: 107).

Table 6.4
Determinants of American Indian Representation among
School Administrators (N=72)

Dependent Variable: Percentage of American Indian School Administrators

Independent Variables	Full Model		Reduced Model	
	Unstandardized Regression Coefficients	Standard Errors	Unstandardized Regression Coefficients	Standard Errors
American Indian Population	0.27*	0.13	0.27*	0.13
American Indian Education	-0.04	0.11		
White Poverty	1.16**	0.23	1.16**	0.22
American Indian School Board Members	0.21#	0.12	0.21#	0.12
Constant	1.69	3.32	0.72	1.29
R^2	0.65			0.65
Adjusted R^2	0.63			0.63
F	32.89**			44.35**

\# $p<.10$
* $p<.05$
** $p<.01$

In regard to African Americans, a 1.0 percentage point increase in school board seats held by African Americans produces a 0.24 percentage point increase in African American administrators. Thus, if one additional person of a five-member school board is African American, there is a 4.8 percentage point increase in African American administrators. (Meier, Stewart, and England 1989: 73). The impact of the political linkage between school board members and administrators seems slightly weaker for American Indians as compared to African Americans, but somewhat stronger than that of Hispanics. Overall, for each minority group, political representation is related to bureaucratic representation.

The strongest determinant of the presence of American Indian administrators in the school districts is white poverty. As white poverty increases, American Indians gain relatively greater access to administrative positions. More specifically, a 1 percentile increase in white poverty produces a 1.16 percentile increase in American Indian administrators. This finding provides strong support for the power theory of intergroup relations, which predicts that white communities would prefer American Indian administrators from middle-class backgrounds over white administrators from lower-class backgrounds.

American Indian Teacher Representation

Although most research focusing on the issue of representative bureaucracy tends to be more interested in upper-level administrators, there has been a growing concern with the representativeness of street-level bureaucrats—such as teachers, policemen, or prosecutors—and their discretion (see Alozie 1996; Hedge, Menzel, and Williams 1988; Lipsky 1980; Meier 1993; Meier and Stewart 1991; Meier, Stewart, and England 1989; Polinard, Wrinkle, and Longoria 1990). The representativeness of teachers is important for a variety of reasons. First, teachers are "political brokers" when it comes to decision making and carrying out policies (Bickel 1982; McIntyre 1990; Schwille, Porter, and Gant 1980; Wirt and Kirst 1989). Teachers are the implementers of school policies (Meier and Stewart 1991; Meier, Stewart, and England 1989). They are at the base level in the educational bureaucracy. As a result, it is teachers who end up with the responsibility of carrying out decisions made by upper-level bureaucrats (administrators) and elected officials (school board members). Furthermore, not only are teachers the implementers of policy, but they are often the developers or makers of educational policy. Moreover, teachers possess considerable discretion that can be used in the process of implementing or making policy decisions (Bickel 1982; Cohen 1982; Meier and Stewart 1991; Meier, Stewart, and England 1989; Schwille, Porter, and Gant 1980; Weick 1976; Wirt and Kirst 1989).

The representativeness of teachers is also important because if teachers are representative of the students, the students are more likely to open up, discuss, be more outgoing, develop relationships, and communicate (Meier and Stewart 1991; Meier, Stewart, and England 1989; Thompson 1976). Previous literature suggests that greater empathy may exist between co-ethnic teachers and students (Polinard, Wrinkle, and Longoria 1990; Smith and June 1982; So 1987). More specifically, in classes with American

Indian teachers, American Indian students are more likely to speak up in class and ask questions than in classes with non-American Indian teachers (Swisher 1990; Swisher and Deyhle 1989; Tonemah 1991). The expectation is that American Indian teachers are more sensitive and receptive to the particular concerns or needs of American Indian students.

A representative bureaucracy at the street level, in this case teachers, implies an openness of the government to all individuals (Meier and Stewart 1991; Meier, Stewart, and England 1989). American Indian teachers can serve as mentors and role models to American Indian students. They illustrate firsthand how to succeed in the education system and demonstrate to young American Indian students that their aspirations to do so are attainable (Cummins 1992; Indian Nations at Risk Task Force 1991; Noley 1992; Reyhner 1992b; Tonemah 1991).

Finally, the representativeness of teachers is important because it fosters an increased awareness and sensitivity to ethnic and racial issues (Meier and Stewart 1991; Meier, Stewart and England 1991; Polinard, Wrinkle, and Longoria 1990; U.S. Commission on Civil Rights 1976). Current trends in education indicate that educators are demonstrating an increased awareness of the needs of children from other cultures, including American Indians (Joshi and Thomas 1991; Reyhner 1992b; Santo 1990; Swisher 1994b). For instance, Stokrocki (1992) notes that white teachers are influenced by their American Indian counterparts to the point that they adopt some strategies used by American Indian teachers. However, this awareness and sensitivity is best generated and maintained by having a representative teacher body. Awareness and sensitivity toward American Indian students is more likely to exist and prosper if there are American Indian teachers among the teaching faculty (Reyhner 1992b; Santo 1990; Stokrocki 1992; Swisher 1994b).

Data in Table 6.1 and Table 6.2 show that American Indians are underrepresented and that American Indian teacher representation is statistically significantly lower than white teacher representation. A more detailed look at American Indian teacher representation is gained by examining the determinants of such representation. The same model used to explain American Indian administrators is used, with the addition of American Indian administrators as an independent variable (see Table 6.5). Two variables are statistically significant—the percentage of American Indians on school boards and the percentage of American Indian administrators in the school district. Overall, the model explains 80 percent of the variance. The effect of American Indian school board representation is such that an additional percentage point is associated with a 0.13 percentage point increase in American Indian teachers. Stated differently, the addition of one American

Table 6.5
Determinants of American Indian Teacher Representation (N=71)

Dependent Variable: Percentage of American Indian Teachers

Independent Variables	Full Model		Reduced Model	
	Unstandardized Regression Coefficients	Standard Errors	Unstandardized Regression Coefficients	Standard Errors
American Indian Population	-0.04	0.07		
American Indian Education	-0.02	0.06		
White Poverty	0.19	0.14		
American Indian Administrators	0.45**	0.06	0.48**	0.05
American Indian School Board Members	0.18**	0.06	0.13**	0.03
Constant	0.52	1.99	1.59	0.64
R^2	0.81			.80
Adjusted R^2	0.80			.80
F	60.89**			154.80**

** $p<.01$

Indian representative to a five-person school board translates into a 2.60 percentage point increase in American Indian teachers, all other things being equal. This finding is in stark contrast to findings for African Americans and Hispanics. In both cases, a significant relationship does not exist between school board representation and teacher representation (but see Polinard, Wrinkle, and Longoria 1990, who found a significant relationship between Mexican American school board members and Mexican American teachers).

The most significant determinant of American Indian teacher representation is the presence of American Indian administrators in the school system. A strong positive relationship exists between administrator representation and teacher representation. A 1.0 percentage point increase in American Indian administrators results in a 0.48 percentage point increase in American Indian teachers. This finding is analogous to that for African Americans. Meier, Stewart, and England (1989: 76) determine that a 1.0 percentage point increase in African American administrators resulted in a 0.44 percentage increase in African American teachers. Interestingly, a 1.0 percentage point increase in Hispanic administrators corresponds to a 0.53 percentage point increase in Hispanic teachers (Meier and Stewart 1991: 110). Thus, the linkage between administrators and teachers is strongest for Hispanics, followed by American Indians, and then African Americans, although they are all relatively close. Furthermore, this finding is consistent with the argument that upper-level bureaucratic representation is related to street-level bureaucratic representation.

LINKING PASSIVE REPRESENTATION WITH ACTIVE REPRESENTATION

Thus far in this chapter we have examined passive American Indian representation on school board and in administrative and teaching positions. Analysis reveals low levels of American Indian representation in the educational policy process, for school board members, administrators, and teachers. In the remainder of this chapter we attempt to determine the extent passive representation results in active representation. Stated differently, does American Indian representation among school board members, administrators, and teachers have an impact on the educational policies that affect American Indian students?

The theory in chapter 3 suggests that academic grouping, discipline, and educational attainment are critical policy impact areas that may be used to analyze the role of American Indian representation. The theory argues that four forces affect second generation discrimination against American Indian students. The variable that links passive and active representation is American Indian political representation. American Indian political representation is expected to decrease the amount of second generation discrimination faced by American Indian students.

Based on the previous research that emphasizes the importance of teachers and their discretionary power as street-level bureaucrats, we argued that teachers are more likely than school board members or administrators to affect second generation discrimination policies.[1] American Indian representation on school boards and among school administrators impact policies that involve second generation discrimination, but teachers have the first opportunity to observe students, to make disciplinary decisions concerning students, and to assess the abilities of students. Furthermore, teachers are in continuous contact with students, whereas administrators and especially school board members have much less contact. The measure of American Indian representation is the percentage of American Indian teachers in the school district.

American Indian resources should decrease the amount of second generation discrimination against American Indian students. American Indians who are politically active can exert pressure on the school district and voice their dissatisfaction with certain policies. Two measures of American Indian political resources are used. The first is the percentage of American Indians in the school district who have graduated from high school. An additional measure is the ratio of American Indian mean family income to white mean family income. The indicator is used to assess the level of American Indian resources compared to white resources.

The model presented in chapter 3 predicts that social class affects second generation discrimination. We argue that second generation discrimination is likely to be influenced by the power thesis of intergroup relations (see Blalock 1967; Feagin 1980; Giles and Evans 1985, 1986). The argument is that discrimination against American Indian students is a function of both race and social class. The specific measure used is the percentage of the white population with an income below the poverty level.

Finally, school district size may affect second generation discrimination. Based on previous research, the effect of district size is predicted to be negative. According to Meier and Stewart (1991), larger school districts are more likely than smaller districts to be professionalized. Increased levels of professionalism lead to greater awareness of the problems of minority students and to an increased recognition that something like second generation discrimination is possible. District size is measured by the total school enrollment.

The dependent variables are the five second generation discrimination policy representation ratios introduced in chapter 4: the EMR class ratio, the LD class ratio, the gifted class ratio, the suspension ratio, and the graduation ratio.[2] In order to avoid problems with extreme cases in the regression analysis, each policy representation ratio is subjected to a log transformation, just as was done in chapter 5 and in previous research (see Meier and Stewart 1991; Meier, Stewart, and England 1989). The log

Table 6.6
Placement of American Indian Students in EMR Classes (N=101)

Dependent Variable: American Indian EMR Ratio

Independent Variables	Full Model		Reduced Model	
	Unstandardized Regression Coefficients	Standard Errors	Unstandardized Regression Coefficients	Standard Errors
American Indian Teachers	-0.27	0.29	-0.26	0.28
American Indian–White Income Ratio	-0.12	0.15		
American Indian Education	0.44	0.35	0.30	0.32
White Poverty	-0.73	0.53	-0.45	0.39
District Size[1]	-0.0030	0.0042		
Constant	0.13	0.11	0.05	0.09
R^2	0.05			0.04
Adjusted R^2	0.01			0.01
F	1.11			1.36

1. Regression coefficients and standard errors for district size are multiplied by 1,000.

transformation changes the interpretation of findings somewhat in that regression slopes now refer to percentage or percentile changes in the dependent variable, rather than to one-unit changes (Tufte 1974).

EMR Classes

Table 6.6 summarizes the effects of American Indian teachers, the American Indian–White income ratio, American Indian education, white poverty, and school district size on the American Indian EMR ratio. Although none of the variables are statistically significant, the regression coefficients, with the single exception of American Indian education, are all in the expected direction. Increases in American Indian teachers, American Indian income, white poverty, and school district size result in decreases in the American Indian EMR representation ratio. A 1.0 percentile increase in American Indian teachers is associated with a 0.27 percentile decrease in American Indian EMR assignments. In comparison, for each 1.0 percentile increase in African American teachers, the African American EMR ratio declines by 0.62 percent in 1984 (Meier, Stewart, England 1989: 96). Although the impact of American Indian teachers is not statistically significant or as strong as the impact resulting from African American teachers, the direction of the impact is consistent with the notion that American Indian teachers use their discretion to increase the access of American Indian students to equal educational opportunities. Moreover, the impact of American Indian teachers appears to be stronger than the impact of Hispanic representation (see Meier and Stewart 1991: 148).

LD Classes

Table 6.7 summarizes the analysis of our five variable second generation discrimination model for the American Indian LD policy ratio. Although only one variable—American Indian–white income ratio—is statistically significant, increases in American Indian teachers and white poverty, as expected, produce decreases in the American Indian LD ratio. The negative relationship between the American Indian–white income ratio and the American Indian LD ratio implies that as American Indian incomes move closer to white incomes, the likelihood of placement of American Indian children in LD classes decreases. An increase of 1.0 percentile in the American Indian–White income ratio results in a 0.18 percentile decrease in the American Indian LD ratio.

Findings here suggest that American Indian children who have parents with higher incomes are less likely to be placed in LD classes. However, another explanation is that the resources of the American Indian community provide a climate that reduces the amount of differential LD assignments. Put differently, income as a political resource seems to be used by American Indian parents to influence school district policies.

Gifted Classes

Chapter 5 shows that American Indians are much less likely to be assigned to gifted classes than are white students. Two variables in Table 6.8 have statistically significant effects on the American Indian gifted ratio—American

Table 6.7
Placement of American Indian Students in LD Classes (N=115)

Dependent Variable: American Indian LD Ratio

Independent Variables	Full Model		Reduced Model	
	Unstandardized Regression Coefficients	Standard Errors	Unstandardized Regression Coefficients	Standard Errors
American Indian Teachers	-0.12	0.23		
American Indian–White Income Ratio	-0.23*	0.12	-0.18#	0.10
American Indian Education	0.30	0.27		
White Poverty	-0.56	0.41		
District Size[1]	0.0012	0.0032		
Constant	0.15	0.08	0.12	0.06
R^2	0.06			0.03
Adjusted R^2	0.02			0.02
F	1.53			3.21#

1. Regression coefficients and standard errors for district size are multiplied by 1,000.

\# $p<.10$
* $p<.05$

Indian teachers and the American Indian–White income ratio, while white poverty is marginally significant. American Indian teachers have the most significant influence on American Indian access to gifted classes. Greater numbers of American Indian teachers results in more American Indian students assigned to gifted classes. An increase of 1.0 percentage point in American Indian teachers coincides with a 1.34 percent increase in the American Indian gifted ratio. This impact is substantially stronger than the

Table 6.8
Placement of American Indian Students in Gifted Classes (N=99)

Dependent Variable: American Indian Gifted Ratio

| | Full Model | | Reduced Model | |
Independent Variables	Unstandardized Regression Coefficients	Standard Errors	Unstandardized Regression Coefficients	Standard Errors
American Indian Teachers	1.11**	0.31	1.34**	0.31
American Indian–White Income Ratio	0.38*	0.18	-0.38*	0.17
American Indian Education	-0.43	0.42		
White Poverty	1.14#	0.64		
District Size[1]	-0.0054	0.0042		
Constant	0.60	0.12	-0.62	0.10
R^2	0.24			0.18
Adjusted R^2	0.20			0.16
F	5.99**			10.64**

1. Regression coefficients and standard errors for district size are multiplied by 1,000

\# $p<.10$
* $p<.05$
** $p<.01$

impact of a 1.0 percentage point increase in Hispanic teachers, which results in a 0.43 percent increase in the Hispanic gifted ratio (Meier and Stewart 1991: 150). Likewise, the effect of American teachers on the American Indian gifted ratio is much greater than the effect of a 1.0 percentage point increase in African American teachers, which in 1984 results in a 0.59 percent increase in the African American gifted ratio (Meier, Stewart, and England 1989: 98-99).

American Indian resources also affect American Indian student assignments to gifted classes. A 1.0 percentile increase in the American Indian–White income ratio is associated with a 0.38 percent increase in American Indian student access to gifted classes. Again income may affect home life, which in turn affects access to gifted classes, but income can also be viewed as a political resource that American Indian parents can use to influence school district policies. Finally, the gifted ratio and white poverty are modestly related. This suggests that in school districts with higher percentages of whites in poverty, American Indians are more equitably represented in gifted classes.

Suspensions

The impacts of the five determinants on the American Indian suspension policy ratio are shown in Table 6.9. All five variables are in the expected direction, except for American Indian education. The statistically significant variables are American Indian teachers, white poverty, and district size. Increases in American Indian teachers, white poverty, and district size are associated with decreases in the American Indian suspension ratio. A 1.0 percentage point increase in American Indian teachers, the most significant variable, corresponds with a 0.48 percentage point decline in the American Indian suspension ratio. The linkage between American Indian teachers and fewer American Indian student suspensions is consistent with the theory of bureaucratic discretion and how such discretion can be used by street-level bureaucrats to the benefit of their constituents (students). For the year 1984, Meier, Stewart, and England (1989: 101) found that a 1.0 percentile increase in African American teachers is associated with a 0.41 percent decrease in the African American suspension ratio. Meier and Stewart (1991: 153) report that a 1.0 percentage point increase in Hispanic representation is associated with a 0.13 percent decline in the Hispanic suspension ratio. The impact of American Indian teachers is more than that for African Americans or Hispanics and lends strong support to the notion that bureaucratic discretion is used to influence policy outputs.

High School Graduation

Graduation rates are influenced by numerous factors beyond the control of the school district, teachers, and administrators in the district. These factors may include, the state of the local economy, dropout programs within the school district, and parental support. In addition, Table 6.10 shows that American Indian teachers have a moderately significant impact on the

Table 6.9
Determinants of Suspended American Indian Students (N=107)

Dependent Variable: American Indian Suspension Ratio

Independent Variables	Full Model		Reduced Model	
	Unstandardized Regression Coefficients	Standard Errors	Unstandardized Regression Coefficients	Standard Errors
American Indian Teachers	- 0.44*	0.23	- 0.48*	0.22
American Indian– White Income Ratio	- 0.12	0.11		
American Indian Education	0.43	0.26		
White Poverty	- 0.77*	0.40	- 0.50#	3.30
District Size[1]	- 0.0065*	0.0032	- 0.0062*	0.0031
Constant	0.20	0.08	0.19	0.04
R^2	0.12			0.09
Adjusted R^2	0.08			0.06
F	3.01*			3.61*

1. Regression coefficients and standard errors for district size are multiplied by 1,000.

\# $p<.10$
* $p<.05$

American Indian graduation ratio. A 1.0 percentile increase in American Indian teachers translates into a 0.38 percent increase in the American Indian graduation ratio. Comparatively, Meier, Stewart, and England (1989: 103) find that a 1.0 percentile increase in African American teachers results in a 0.18 percent increase in the African American student graduation ratio. Meier and Stewart (1991: 156) report that a 1.0 percentage point increase in Hispanic representation produces an increase of 0.12 percent in the Hispanic graduation ratio. The impact of American Indian teachers is larger

Table 6.10
Determinants of American Indian High School Graduates (N=107)

Dependent Variable: American Indian Graduation Ratio

Independent Variables	Full Model		Reduced Model	
	Unstandardized Regression Coefficients	Standard Errors	Unstandardized Regression Coefficients	Standard Errors
American Indian Teachers	0.43#	0.23	0.38#	0.22
American Indian– White Income Ratio	0.01	0.12		
American Indian Education	-0.06	0.32		
White Poverty	-0.18	0.42		
District Size[1]	-0.0001	0.0034		
Constant	-0.13	0.10	-0.15	0.03
R^2	0.03			0.03
Adjusted R^2	0.01			0.02
F	0.73			2.92#

1. Regression coefficients and standard errors for district size are multiplied by 1,000.

\# $p < .10$

than that found for African Americans or Hispanics. Similarly, to African American and Hispanic teachers, findings here suggest that American Indian teachers are good role models for American Indian students. Moreover, findings imply that American Indian teachers exercise bureaucratic discretion to assist and encourage American Indian students and thus mitigate the effects of second generation discrimination.

Second Generation Discrimination Factor

To this point we have examined the impact of our five variable policy determinant model separately for each of the five second generation discrimination policy ratios—EMR, LD, gifted, suspensions, and graduation rates. Next, we create a single measure of second generation discrimination based on all five of our dependent variables, i.e., policy ratios. We employ a factor analysis technique in order to combine the five variables. Factor analysis allows the common variation shared by the five indicators to be examined. In order to tap this common variation the five indicators are factor analyzed (see Table 5.3). A single significant dimension results from the analysis. Each of the individual measures loaded in the correct direction on this single factor. Higher scores on the factor indicate greater amounts of second generation discrimination. Similar to the analyses performed for the previous five measures of second generation discrimination, the new second generation discrimination factor is now used as the dependent variable in a multiple regression analysis.

Table 6.11 reveals that all the variables have the predicted impact on the second generation discrimination policy factor except for the American Indian education variable. This variable is not statistically significant in the reduced model, nor is district size. Analogous to the findings for several of the single second generation discrimination measures, American Indian teachers provide the most statistically significant effect on the second generation discrimination policy indicator. As the number of American Indian teachers increases, the incidence of second generation discrimination among American Indian students decreases. A 1.0 percentage point increase in American Indian teachers corresponds with a 2.29 percent decrease in the second generation discrimination factor index.

Increases in white poverty provide modest decreases in second generation discrimination among American Indians. Put differently, in school districts with larger lower-class white populations, discrimination against American Indians is mitigated. This finding supports the power theory of intergroup relations of Giles, Evans, and Feagin and views discrimination against American Indian students as a function of both race and social class. It also represents a social-class bias in the educational system because poor whites are also discriminated against.

Table 6.11
Determinants of the Second Generation Discrimination Factor
for American Indian Students (N=89)

Dependent Variable: Second Generation Discrimination Factor Scores for
American Indian Students

Independent Variables	Full Model		Reduced Model	
	Unstandardized Regression Coefficients	Standard Errors	Unstandardized Regression Coefficients	Standard Errors
American Indian Teacher	-2.09*	0.96	-2.29*	0.94
American Indian-White Income Ratio	-0.80	0.48		
American Indian Education	2.66*	1.25	1.81	1.22
White Poverty	-4.86*	1.97	-2.32#	1.34
District Size[1]	-0.0056	0.0127		
Constant	0.59	0.39	0.05	0.32
R^2	0.21			0.14
Adjusted R^2	0.16			0.11
F	4.66*			5.02*

1. Regression coefficients and standard errors for district size are multiplied by 1,000.

\# $p < .10$
* $p < .05$

SUMMARY OF SECOND GENERATION DISCRIMINATION MEASURES

Analyses presented in this chapter show that the most consistent
determinant mitigating second generation discrimination against American
Indian students is the presence of American Indian teachers in school
districts. For each of the five policy ratios the impact of American Indian

teachers on second generation discrimination is in the predicted direction. American Indian teachers reduce the amount of second generation discrimination for each policy ratio. More American Indian teachers are associated with proportionately fewer American Indian students placed in EMR and LD classes. American Indian teachers have a positive impact on the enrollment of American Indian students in gifted classes. Increases in American Indian teachers also result in lower disparities in the number of American Indian students suspended. Finally, American Indian teachers have a positive impact on the number of American Indian students who graduate.

The political resources of the American Indian community have mixed effects on second generation discrimination. Increases in American Indian income levels, as expected, correspond with decreases in second generation discrimination. Increases in American Indian incomes result in significantly lower American Indian LD class ratios and substantially higher American Indian gifted class ratios. American Indian education did not significantly influence any of the policy ratio measures.

For the most part, white poverty had the hypothesized affect, although the impact was only modest. Social class plays a role in American Indian student access to equal educational opportunities. The more poor whites in the district, the less American Indians experience second generation discrimination. Just like American Indian political resources, social class is not as significant of a factor in reducing second generation discrimination as is the presence of American Indian teachers.

District size does not have a consistent influence on the second generation discrimination measures. However, it did exhibit one significant relationship. Larger school districts suspended American Indian students in proportionately smaller numbers than smaller districts.

Similar to the findings for Hispanics (Meier and Stewart 1991), this model of second generation discrimination does not predict as well for American Indians as it does for African Americans (Meier, Stewart, and England 1989). Nevertheless, Tables 6.6 through 6.11 demonstrate that American Indian representation in schools is vitally important and that *American Indian teachers do provide active representation.*

CONCLUSION

This chapter analyzes the impact of American Indian representation on second generation discrimination. First, the passive representation of American Indians on school boards and in administrative and teaching positions was found to be low. However, when American Indians have political representation on school boards, American Indian representation in the educational bureaucracy increases. That is, the number of American Indian administrators and teachers increases. Likewise, American Indian representation in administrative positions has significant and positive effects on American Indian representation in teaching positions in public schools.

Passive representation was linked to active representation. Specifically, American Indian teachers provide active representation for American Indian students. We conclude that American Indian teachers produce policy outputs that benefit American Indian students and thus increase their access to equal educational opportunities.

NOTES

1. The interactive effect of American Indian school board representation and American Indian teacher representation was tested. In one test the American Indian teacher variable and the American Indian school board variable were included with the interaction variable (see Friedrich 1982 in support of using multiplicative terms). The interaction variable and the American Indian school board variable were nonsignificant in every case, whereas the American Indian teachers were significant in the same dependent variables they had been before. When just the interaction variable was included in the models, it was not significant in every case. Identical findings were made when the interactive effect of American Indian administrators and American Indians teachers was tested.

2. Representation ratios calculated as the proportion of American Indian students assigned or disciplined divided by the proportion of non–American Indian students were tested in Tables 6.6 through 6.11. The results were not significantly different from the ratios that are presented, which are calculated as the proportion of American Indian students assigned or disciplined divided by the proportion of all students so assigned or disciplined.

Chapter 7

Mitigating Second Generation Discrimination: Lessons from Case Studies

Chapter 6 provided a quantitative aggregate analysis of political forces that influence second generation discrimination among American Indian students. These political forces include the presence of American Indian teachers in public schools, the resources of the American Indian community, and poverty among whites. Our research as well as previous research on second generation discrimination suggests that of all factors associated with second generation discrimination, minority teachers have the greatest impact on second generation discrimination. Increases in minority teachers result in *decreases* in the amount of second generation discrimination endured by African American students (Meier, Stewart, and England 1989), Hispanic students (Meier and Stewart 1991), and American Indian students (see chapter 6). However, studies generally fail to specify exactly how and why minority teachers make such a difference. Specific within-school policies and practices (e.g., programs, curricula, and teaching methods) that either facilitate or constrain second generation discrimination have not been thoroughly studied. This chapter attempts to address this research gap.

This chapter on second generation discrimination among American Indians presents the findings from five in-depth case studies, two from Oklahoma and three from Alabama, and suggests strategies and policies that may be used to combat the deleterious impact of second generation discrimination. The use of the case study methodology allows us to extend the literature on second generation discrimination and thus enhance and enrich the overall understanding of second generation discrimination beyond that presented by other studies, which provide only quantitative, aggregate findings (see

Meier and Stewart 1991; Meier, Stewart, and England 1989; Polinard, Wrinkle, and Longoria 1990). In short, with these case studies we augment the quantitative aggregate analyses presented in chapters 5 and 6.

The chapter is organized into four sections. First, we identify within-school variables that are suggested by previous literature to significantly affect second generation discrimination. Second, we outline data and methods used for the case studies. Third, we present case study findings, beginning with two case studies in Oklahoma, followed by three case studies in Alabama. Finally, we conclude and discuss implications of the case studies.

WITHIN-SCHOOL FACTORS AFFECTING SECOND GENERATION DISCRIMINATION: A REVIEW OF FINDINGS

There are a number of possible factors or variables that previous studies suggest may have an influence on a school district's treatment of minority students. Before discussing data, research methods, and findings, we outline some of these factors, since they represent the theoretical background that guide our interviews in the case studies.

American Indian Teachers

Previous research on second generation discrimination has determined that African American teachers (Meier, Stewart, and England 1989), Hispanic teachers (Meier and Stewart 1991), and Mexican American teachers (Polinard, Wrinkle, and Longoria 1990) produce positive results for minority students. Increases in the numbers of these minority teachers result in less second generation discrimination for minority students. As part of our larger study of American Indians and second generation discrimination, the same results occur: More American Indian teachers result in less second generation discrimination for American Indian students (see chapter 6). However, this finding is made at the aggregate level and is the product of quantitative analysis. It is also important to see if the same results occur at the micro or individual school district level.

Additionally, previous research that points out the importance of minority teachers (Meier and Stewart 1991; Meier, Stewart, and England 1989, 1991; Polinard, Wrinkle, and Longoria 1990) puts forth several hypotheses as to why the minority teacher is important. These reasons include the following: (1) Contact and communication between lower-level bureaucrats (teachers) and clients (students) is often facilitated if the bureaucrats are representative of the clients (Thompson 1976); (2) greater empathy may exist between co-ethnic teachers and students (Smith and June 1982; So 1987); (3) a representative bureaucracy at the street level, in this case among teachers, implies an openness of the bureaucracy to all individuals, in which case different minority teachers can serve as role models to their respective minority students (Meier and Stewart 1991; Meier, Stewart, and England 1989) and (4) the representativeness of teachers might foster an increased awareness and sensitivity to ethnic and racial issues (Meier, Stewart and England 1989, 1991; U.S. Commission on Civil Rights 1976). The case study part of this research will allow us to test these hypotheses with interviews and direct observations. Besides determining if American Indian teachers are important and why, the case studies are designed to examine specific within-school policies and practices that either facilitate or constrain second generation discrimination.

Cooperative Learning

A wealth of research emphasizes the point that different teaching methods affect the quality of education children receive. Put differently, research suggests that certain teaching methods—street-level bureaucratic behavior— influence the access of students to equal educational opportunities. For example, research suggests in-school alternatives to suspensions (Froyen 1993; Radin 1988; Williams 1979; Wolfgang 1995) and advocates the "mainstreaming" of minority children (see Beare 1981; Jones 1976; Slavin 1986, 1988, 1989). Indeed, there are alternatives to segregating students through academic grouping that are easy to implement and that have proven to be effective pedagogical tools both for students with low abilities and students with high abilities. These alternatives are referred to as cooperative learning techniques (Johnson, Johnson, Holubec, and Roy 1984; Putnam 1993; Rynders et al. 1993; Slavin 1980, 1981, 1982, 1986, 1988, 1989; Slavin and Dickle 1981) and require the mainstreaming of students across the full range of racial, ethnic, ability, and gender groups in the classrooms.

The research on strategies or techniques of cooperative learning is voluminous. Some of the cooperative learning models, researched at the Johns Hopkins University Center for the Social Organization of Schools, are Teams-Games-Tournament (TGT), Student Teams-Achievement Divisions (STAD), Jigsaw I and II, group investigation, and small-group teaching, just to mention a few. Regardless of the particular manifestation used, cooperative learning strategies foster school integration by allowing for multiple-ability instruction and equal status of students. Some of the other advantages highlighted by research on cooperative learning include significant increases in student achievement; better recollection of factual material; improvement in the social outcomes of schooling, such as intergroup relations and attitudes toward mainstreamed students; less defensiveness among the students; increase in the ability to see situations from other view points; less threatening classroom environment, which leads to more student participation; increase in students' responsibility for their own learning; and positive effects on the self-esteem of students.

The educational literature suggests that minorities, including American Indians, perform better and are less likely to be discriminated against when teachers create cooperative learning environments as opposed to competitive classrooms (Brown 1980; Gordon and Boseker 1984; Rehyner 1992b; Shutiva 1991; Slavin and Dickle 1981; Slavin 1989; Stokrocki 1992; Swisher 1990; Swisher and Deyhle 1989; Tonemah 1991).

Several questions remain. Are cooperative learning strategies used and do they work? Are there other educational strategies and policies that school officials use to impede second generation discrimination? Do personnel within school districts perceive minority teachers and cooperative learning as important? If they do, which of the factors do they perceive as most important? These questions helped guide us when we went to the field to conduct our case studies. Before we discuss findings from our field work, case study data, methods, and procedures are outlined.

DATA AND METHODS

Advantages and Uses of Qualitative Research

Most second generation discrimination studies either use a quantitative, aggregate, comparative approach involving a large number of school districts (Meier and Stewart 1991; Meier, Stewart, and England 1989; Polinard, Wrinkle, and Longoria 1990) or have taken the form of qualitative case studies (Metz 1978; Oakes 1985; Rosenbaum 1976; U.S. Commission on Civil Rights 1977), rather than employ a combination of the two approaches. Although both of these approaches provide essential information, either one without the other omits vital facts (see Goggin 1986). A quantitative aggregate analysis, though easily generalized to many districts, always leaves unexplained variation and sometimes involves using somewhat gross measures; thus, the phenomenon is not completely understood. For example, minority teachers may be associated with less second generation discrimination, but the teaching methods used by these teachers are unknown. In other words, the actual behavior of Lipsky's (1980) street-level bureaucrats, in this case teachers, has not been examined in the study. Specific within-school policies and practices (e.g., programs and teaching methods) that either facilitate or constrain resegregation are not included in the model. Furthermore, quantitative aggregate analyses cannot take into account the unique or unusual conditions that are found in almost every school district. Conversely, qualitative research such as case studies tap these unique conditions, but extreme caution must be taken when generalizing results to other locations.

Our research is based on both techniques—quantitative aggregate analysis and qualitative case studies—in order to gain the advantages of each (King, Keohane, and Verba 1994; Goggin 1986). First, the incidence and number of variables explaining second generation discrimination for American Indian students are studied. This part of the analysis was presented in chapters 5 and 6. Second, case studies are undertaken to better understand the dynamics of second generation discrimination (chapter 7). This combination of methods extends the literature on second generation discrimination and enhances and enriches our overall understanding of second generation discrimination. Additionally, the case studies should help establish a knowledge base needed to identify strategies for mitigating second generation discrimination.

Selection and Description of Cases

Five case studies are summarized here, two from Oklahoma and three from Alabama. The two Oklahoma case studies were conducted in the spring of 1995 and predated the sponsorship of the case study component of our research through a travel grant. Oklahoma ranks second among the states in American Indian population. Oklahoma is also the home state oi the researchers, thus facilitating ease of travel and tremendously reducing research costs. Within the state, we identified two school districts that were part of our larger 128 school district sample. The school districts chosen in Oklahoma were the Clinton Public Schools and the Watonga Public Schools.

Three Alabama school districts are also included as case studies. Travel support for these case studies was provided through a research grant. The case studies were conducted in the fall of 1996. The school districts serving as case study sites in Alabama are the Jackson County Public Schools, the Lawrence County Public Schools, and the DeKalb County Public Schools. Unlike the two Oklahoma case studies that were part of our 128 school district sample and selected primarily because of location, the criterion used to select the three Alabama school districts is their favorable second generation discrimination factor scores. Of the 128 school districts included in the sample, the second generation discrimination factor scores calculated in chapter 6 show that the three Alabama school districts selected for case studies rank in the top ten school districts that show "good" treatment of American Indian students (e.g., higher percentage of American Indian students in gifted classes and higher graduation rates, fewer American Indian suspensions, and fewer American Indians in EMR and LD classes). These school districts were "statistical outliers" and had much less second generation discrimination than one would predict based on our theoretical model tested in chapter 6. In fact, Jackson County and DeKalb County rank one and three, respectively, on the factor scores.

In sum, all five school districts are part of our larger study sample. The two Oklahoma case studies were chosen primarily because of their location and were not chosen based on any prior knowledge of representation of American Indians on school boards or in administrative and teaching positions. Additionally, we did not examine, nor do we report, second generation discrimination policy ratios (for EMR, LD, and gifted classes, suspensions, and graduation rates) for the districts prior to performing the case studies. On the other hand, the three Alabama case studies were chosen purely for statistical reasons. Based on our regression model, they are outliers and represent "model" schools in terms of promoting equal educational opportunities. A brief introduction to each school district follows.

Clinton, Oklahoma

Clinton is located in Custer County, which was part of the original Cheyenne-Arapaho Reservation established by a treaty in 1867. Clinton was part of the 3.5 million acres of land opened for settlement by the land run of April 19, 1892. The city was established largely as a result of the westward expansion of the railroads. The Rock Island Railroad completed its east-west line to present-day Clinton, then called Washita Junction, in 1903. A special act of Congress allowed four American Indians to sell half of each of their 160 acre allotments to create the Clinton townsite (Oklahoma Department of Libraries 1991).

Today, the economy is allied with oil and gas prices, as Clinton lies atop the rich Anadarko Basin. In addition to the oil and gas industry, Clinton is heavily influenced by the agricultural and farming industry. Clinton is a small community with a population of 10,386. This population is fairly diverse: About 74 percent is white, 10 percent is Hispanic, 8 percent is American Indian, and 7 percent is African American. The community is fairly representative of upper-, middle-, and lower-income classes, although 56 percent of the American Indian families live in poverty.

The Clinton school district has five public schools: one high school (Clinton High School), one middle school (Clinton Middle School), and three elementary schools (Nance Elementary, Southwest Elementary, and Washington Elementary). With regard to school funding, the revenue per pupil in Clinton is $3,273. Although this amount is approximately $1,200 less than the school district sample mean of $4,442, it is much closer to Oklahoma's average revenue per pupil which is $3,779. The total school district enrollment is 2,066, with white students representing approximately 60 percent of this total. Hispanics make up around 19 percent of the student body, while American Indians and African Americans, respectively, are almost 10 percent of the school district enrollment. One hundred thirty-three teachers are employed by the Clinton school district.

Watonga, Oklahoma

Watonga, the county seat of Blaine County, is named for Watangaa, or Black Coyote, an Arapaho Indian leader (Oklahoma Department of Libraries 1991). Watonga is a rural community located about 50 miles northwest of Oklahoma City and has a population of 4,584. The ethnic breakdown of the population shows that about 80 percent is white, 8 percent is American Indian, 8 percent is African American, and 3 percent is Hispanic. This population base has been gradually decreasing as a result of few job or career opportunities. Most of the employment prospects are with a carpet factory, a cheese factory, or farming and agriculturally related fields. Thus, the majority of the people are blue-collar and only a small percentage of the population is college educated.

The Watonga school district has three public schools: one high school, one middle school, and one elementary school. With regard to school funding, the revenue per pupil in Watonga is $3,188. Although this amount is about $1,200 less than the sample mean of $4,442, it is much closer to Oklahoma's average revenue per pupil, which is $3,779. The total school district enrollment is 1,023, with white students representing approximately 60 percent of this total. American Indians make up 18 percent of the student body, whereas African Americans and Hispanics, are 12 and 5 percent of the school district enrollment, respectively. Sixty-eight teachers are employed by the Watonga school district.

Jackson County, Alabama

Jackson County, the third largest of Alabama's sixty-seven counties, is located in northeastern Alabama at the foothills of the Appalachian Mountains. The county is named for frontiersman and president Andrew Jackson, who was primarily responsible for the relocation of many southern Indian tribes (e.g., Cherokee, Creek, Choctaw, and Chickasaw) that occupied northern Alabama. Jackson County has a population of approximately 50,000 people. The ethnic breakdown of the population shows that 92.5 percent is white, with approximately 20 percent of those with some percentage of American Indian ancestry. Most of the employment prospects are with agriculture, the textile and apparel industry, and the tourist industry. The unemployment rate for Jackson County is 9.1 percent. The median household income is $25,023 with about 20 percent considered to be below poverty.

Jackson County schools employ over 400 teachers in seventeen primary schools. These include six K–12 schools, six K–8 schools, two 5–8 schools, two K–4 schools, and one 9–12 school. With regard to school funding, expenditures per pupil in Jackson County are $4,729, which is about $300 more than the school district sample mean of $4,384. The total school district enrollment is about 6,600 of which 15 percent are recognized as American Indian students.

Lawrence County, Alabama

Lawrence County, centered in a major industrial hub, is located in the northwestern section of Alabama. Lawrence County has a population of approximately 32,000 people. The ethnic breakdown of the population shows that about 77 percent is white, 15 percent is black, 7 percent is American Indian, and 1 percent is Hispanic. Most of the employment prospects are with manufacturing.

Lawrence County schools employ nearly 400 teachers in seven primary schools. With regard to school funding, expenditures per pupil in Lawrence County are $4,902, which is about $500 more than the school district sample mean of $4,384. The total school district enrollment is 6,500, of which 25 percent are recognized as American Indian students.

DeKalb County, Alabama

DeKalb County, located in northeastern Alabama, was once a part of the territory occupied by the Cherokee Indian Nation. As the immigration of settlers into the Cherokee country increased, friction between the two races escalated. The Treaty of New Echota, signed in 1835, ceded the Cherokee lands in Alabama to the federal government and forced most of the American Indian population westward. DeKalb County has a population of approximately 56,000 people, with over 70 percent residing in rural areas. The ethnic breakdown of the population shows that 97 percent is white, with almost 30 percent of those with some percentage of American Indian ancestry. Most of the employment prospects are with manufacturing (e.g., the county seat is Fort Payne, recognized as the "Sock Capital of the World"), farming, and forestry. The median household income is $23,485, with about 20 percent considered to be below poverty.

DeKalb County schools employ about 400 teachers in twelve primary schools. These include eight K–12 schools and four K–8 schools. With regard to school funding, expenditures per pupil in Lawrence County are $4,674, which is about $300 more than the school district sample mean of $4,384. The total school district enrollment is 7,300, of which 25 percent are recognized as American Indian students.

Procedures Used for the Case Studies

Similar procedures were used to gather data for all five case studies.[1] First, permission from the superintendent of schools for each school district to do the case studies was obtained. School superintendents gave permission to use the name of the school districts. Second, interviews with both superintendents were conducted during which assurances were made that they and their faculty and staff members would have anonymity. In addition to superintendents, the following school personnel were interviewed in Oklahoma: Every school administrator (these included principals and assistant principals, as well as the administrators in charge of any American Indian programs), teachers (these included several white teachers, all the American Indian teachers in Clinton, and several African American teachers), counselors (these included the American Indian counselor in each of the school districts, as well as several white counselors), an American Indian school board member in Clinton, an African American school board member in Watonga, and a group of seven American Indian students in Clinton. Access to a similar group of students in Watonga could not be arranged. In all, twenty-five different people in the Clinton school district and fifteen in the Watonga school district were interviewed.

For the three Alabama case studies, superintendents, school administrators (principals, assistant principals, and directors of the American Indian Education Programs), and a large number of teachers were interviewed. In all, 100 different school district personnel in Jackson County, 99 school district personnel in Lawrence County, and 98 school district personnel in DeKalb County were interviewed.

Interview procedures are similar to those used by Kingdon (1989) in his interviews with U.S. congresspersons to ascertain what influences their voting decisions. Superintendents, administrators, and teachers were asked an open-ended question in which they were instructed to suggest factors or variables that might explain, or at least influence, the school district's treatment of American Indian students. In Kingdon's words, this allows individuals the opportunity to comment "spontaneously." Presumably, if the person being interviewed mentions a factor or gives an explanation spontaneously, then the factor is salient to the person.

In contrast, if an interviewee does not respond with any particular factor, is vague, noncommittal, or not definitive, he or she is, in Kingdon's words, "prompted"; that is, possible influential factors are suggested (e.g., American Indian teachers, cooperative learning, or an American Indian Education program). This allows the person being interviewed to mention a factor or give an explanation in response to a question. Interviewees are prompted by questions such as these: (1) Do you think the presence of American Indian teachers and/or administrators plays a role in the school district's treatment of American Indian students? (2) Do you think that the use of cooperative learning techniques plays a role in the school district's treatment of American Indian students? (3) Is there something about the community in which the school district lies that may influence the school district's treatment of American Indian students? (4) Do you think the presence of an American Indian Education program plays a role in the school district's treatment of American Indian students? Thus, each potential factor is coded in three possible ways: mentioned spontaneously, mentioned in response to a question (that is, having some importance in the school district's treatment of its American Indians, but not enough to be mentioned spontaneously), or no apparent impact on the treatment (at least in the mind of the person being interviewed).

FINDINGS OF THE CASE STUDIES

Two Case Studies in Oklahoma

An Analysis of Important Factors Affecting the Treatment of American Indian Students

The results of our coding scheme for the two Oklahoma case studies appear in Table 7.1. In the Clinton school district it seems that two factors—American Indian teachers and cooperative learning—are believed to account for, or at least to influence, the treatment of American Indians in the school district. Both of these variables are on the minds of the personnel interviewed, although interviewees are likely to mention spontaneously American Indian teachers somewhat more than cooperative learning. Both explanations received far more spontaneous mentions (at least twice as many) than any other variable. Moreover, all interviewees cite the influences of American Indian teachers and cooperative learning either in a spontaneous mention or in regard to a specific question. Apparently, the two factors that Clinton

Table 7.1
Possible Explanations for School District Treatment of American Indian Students: Clinton and Watonga

Clinton (N=25)

Mentioned	American Indian Teacher	Cooperative Learning	Multicultural Club	Community
Spontaneously	80	68	32	28
In Response to a Question	20	32	56	56
Not a Factor	0	0	12	16

Watonga (N=15)

Mentioned	American Indian Counselor	Minority Teacher	Cooperative Learning	American Indian Club	Community
Spontaneously	73	67	40	53	20
In Response to a Question	27	33	53	27	33
Not a Factor	0	0	7	20	47

Note: Table reports percentages.

school district personnel believe explain the district's treatment of American Indian students are American Indian teachers and the use of cooperative learning, followed by the district's multicultural club and community support.

In the Watonga school district, the most often spontaneously mentioned factor positively affecting American Indian students is the American Indian counselor. The next most frequently and spontaneously mentioned factors are the presence of minority teachers, cooperative learning, the American Indian Club, and community support. Watonga has only one American Indian counselor, and this person does not hold a teaching position. Nevertheless, school district personnel believe this person plays a crucial role in ensuring that American Indian students receive equal educational opportunities in the school district (on the importance of school counselors see Smith and June 1982).

That non–American Indian minority teachers (African Americans and Hispanics) are spontaneously mentioned as important factors in securing American Indian equal educational opportunities as frequently as they are is a very interesting finding. One might interpret the power theory of intergroup relations argued by Feagin (1980), Giles and Evans (1985, 1986), and Meier and Stewart (1991) to suggest that minority teachers in Watonga, African American and Hispanic teachers, would be more likely to protect their own respective minority students and not be as interested in protecting American Indian students. Viewed as a zero-sum situation, one group of minority teachers takes care of its own group of minority students. However, the finding that minority teachers take care of minority students regardless of race or ethnicity corresponds with Browning, Marshall, and Tabb's (1984) incorporation thesis, which stresses cooperation of minority groups instead of competition.

One other finding regarding the minority teacher issue is surprising. No one in Clinton spontaneously mentioned the presence of African American or Hispanic teachers as a possible explanation for the districts' treatment of American Indian students, whereas ten out of fifteen (67 percent) did in Watonga. Instead, school personnel in Clinton talk about *American Indian teachers* and their influence. Possible explanations for this finding might include the following. First, since Watonga has no American Indian teachers, respondents who believe that American Indian students' treatment has anything to do with minority teachers must mention African American and/ or Hispanic (minority) teachers. Second, Watonga's American Indian club is sponsored by an African American man who, according to people interviewed, has a "great reputation" and has been teaching for over fifteen years within the district. Indeed, he received particularly high praise from the American Indian counselor and the high school principal. Conversely, in Clinton there is no American Indian club, although there is a multicultural club that is currently sponsored by an American Indian woman. Third, another possible reason minority teachers may have been mentioned in Watonga and not in Clinton involves the composition of the two school boards. Watonga has four Anglos and one African American on the school board, whereas Clinton has four Anglos and one American Indian on the school board. In the interviews with the American Indian school board member in Clinton and the African American school board member in Watonga, they each spontaneously mentioned their respective minority teachers. We believe that the composition of these school boards influences teachers and thus the districts' treatment of American Indians.

In regard to cooperative learning, Watonga school personnel believe that cooperative learning is an important factor in the school district's treatment of American Indians, although not nearly as important as it is perceived to be in Clinton. In Watonga, 93 percent of the interviewees either mention cooperative learning spontaneously (40 percent) or when prompted (53 percent). This total is higher than that for the impact of Watonga's American Indian club (80 percent), although the club is mentioned more spontaneously (53 percent) than cooperative learning. Finally, characteristics about the community are mentioned as important about half of the time, even when prompted. Thus, in the Watonga school district it seems that the American Indian counselor and the minority teachers are two factors that school district personnel believe explain their district's treatment of American Indians, followed by the district's use of cooperative learning and its American Indian club.

Another method of determining explanations for the treatment of American Indian students in the two school districts is to assess the *importance* of each factor or explanation. This can be accomplished by coding the apparent overall importance of the factor or explanation, regardless of the number of times it is mentioned in the interview. In this case, the interviewee's comments relative to each factor are coded into two categories: The factor was likely to be either important or unimportant in the treatment of their American Indian students. The results of this coding scheme appear in Table 7.2.

The patterns for each of the school districts are similar to the ones found in Table 7.1. For the Clinton school district, American Indian teachers and cooperative learning are important in every interview. This is followed by the multicultural club and the community. Both are thought to be important by over half the interviewees. In the Watonga school district, the American Indian counselor and minority teachers are important to all respondents. Again, cooperative learning and the American Indian club are important at similar rates, whereas the community is not.

Tables 7.1 and 7.2 document and establish the perceived importance of the American Indian teacher and the use of cooperative learning in the Clinton school district and also the importance of the American Indian counselor and the minority (African American and Hispanic) teachers in the Watonga school district. Having identified these factors as important, a further discussion of each is merited, since the tables do not show *why* the factors are perceived as important.

Table 7.2
Importance of the Possible Explanations for School District Treatment of American Indian Students: Clinton and Watonga

Clinton (N=25)				
Mentioned	American Indian Teacher	Cooperative Learning	Multicultural Club	Community
Important	100	100	64	60
Unimportant	0	0	36	40

Watonga (N=15)				
Mentioned	American Indian Counselor	Minority Teacher	Cooperative Learning	American Indian Club	Community
Important	100	100	67	67	47
Unimportant	0	0	33	33	53

Note: Table reports percentages.

American Indian Teachers and Counselors and Other Minority Teachers

Based on the interviews in both Oklahoma school districts there seem to be several reasons why American Indian teachers and/or counselor as well as other minority teachers (African American and Hispanic) are important factors explaining the districts' treatment of American Indians. First, almost all interviewees spontaneously mentioned these teachers as role models for American Indian students. One of the American Indian teachers interviewed in Clinton said, "I would certainly hope that all of the American Indian students see me, as well as all of the other American Indian teachers as good role models, and I think they [American Indian students] do. I would like to think that we [the American Indian teachers] have a positive impact on the educational quality received by our American Indian students." Similar comments are made by other American Indian teachers in Clinton. Furthermore, the American Indian counselor elaborated on this idea by mentioning that she thought, "American Indian students look up to American

Indian teachers as role models due to the fact that the students know that the teachers have overcome some of the same obstacles or barriers and had to deal with some of the same problems as they [American Indian students] face." The counselor went on to say that this was one reason why she encourages American Indian students to view American Indian teachers as role models.

Many of the white teachers in Clinton believe that the district's American Indian teachers have a positive impact on American Indian students. One teacher even thought that Clinton has many teachers who are not classified as American Indians, but are likely to be part American Indian. She argues this is also beneficial to American Indian students. Another teacher stated that she knows that many of the surrounding school districts do not have any American Indians on their teaching staffs, although the districts have even higher enrollments of American Indians than the Clinton school district. She suggests that the presence of American Indian teachers improves the treatment of American Indians in the Clinton school district, especially since Clinton's American Indian teachers are so highly trained and possess a great deal of experience.

Similarly, the superintendent in Clinton argues that the training and experience of American Indian teachers helps earn the respect of other teachers. This respect helps the non–American Indian teachers develop an increased awareness and sensitivity to ethnic and racial issues, especially those important to American Indian students. This idea represents another reason, besides acting as role models, why American Indian teachers and counselors are viewed as important in the treatment of American Indian students.

Several white teachers in each district allude to their respect for their American Indian, African American, and Hispanic counterparts. They also point out how this respect leads to an encouraged responsiveness and sensitivity toward American Indian students' needs. These teachers recall often consulting with American Indian teachers or counselors, as well as other minority teachers, about issues that might be helpful for American Indian students. Moreover, the white teachers, especially in Clinton, mention that sometimes following these discussions they adopt some of the topics and strategies used by American Indian teachers. For instance, one teacher states, "I think that sometimes if we [the white teachers] can't motivate the American Indian students, or any student for that matter, beginning the moment they walk into our classrooms, then we just let them drift aimlessly without pushing or challenging them. Often our [the white teachers'] expectations are not what they should be. However, because of the respect we have for our American Indian colleagues and the concern that they have helped to foster, many of us will discuss situations involving American Indian students with our American Indian teachers or counselors. The American Indian teachers and counselor remind the other teachers that we need to keep high expectations of our American Indian students in order to receive higher quality work and in order for them to a receive a higher quality education."

The American Indian counselor agrees that American Indian teachers have increased the awareness and concern for American Indian issues. She brought up an interesting development, which she argues demonstrates the increased sensitivity. "In the past, say over ten years ago, our white teachers would come to me and ask me to do something about a particular American Indian child in their class. Now, as the school district has hired more American Indian teachers and also over time, most of the white teachers will inquire about why the child is acting a particular way. The white teachers are more concerned with the reasons behind the American Indian students' behavior and are more interested in working with them, instead of just turning the students over to me."

Likewise, in the Watonga school district, several teachers describe what has happened since the employment of the American Indian counselor. One white teacher seems to put it most eloquently when he states, "Ten or fifteen years ago, before the American Indian counselor was hired and raised all the teachers' sensitivity and helped us become more conscious of our actions, we were certainly very discriminatory, much more so than today, of our American Indian students. You would have seen a totally different picture here ten years ago. However, once the counselor appeared many things started to slowly change. It is not like it happened overnight, it did take some time, but changes definitely have taken place. This is due, in large part, to him [the American Indian counselor] pointing out some of our subtle biases and informing us of some of our past mistakes and problems. He really helped us—the school district and especially some of the white teachers—to open our eyes and consider the consequences of our actions or behaviors."

A principal in Watonga describes how the American Indian counselor increased sensitivity among the teachers about the needs and concerns of American Indian students by listing some of the job responsibilities of the counselor, as well as some of his accomplishments. The duties of the counselor include: promoting school attendance of the American Indian students, which requires picking up approximately twenty students each morning in a school van; going into students' homes and counseling with parents, especially if a student has discipline problems; tutoring students; emphasizing that students be on time and submit assignments; and encouraging student participation in extracurricular activities. The principal feels that the counselor, stays "on top of the American Indian kids and makes sure they give school their best shot." She describes the counselor as a "step-parent," while the superintendent thinks of him as a "surrogate parent" to many of the American Indian students. With this in mind, it is not surprising that many American Indian students look up to the counselor and view him as a positive role model.

Some of the more notable accomplishments made by the counselor and mentioned by others include the development and organization of the school Indian Club, which some staff in Watonga consider a manifestation of the district's commitment to being aware and sympathetic to American Indian issues; the large number of American Indian students involved in extracurricular activities; and the exemplary attendance levels of American Indian students. The superintendent notes that the counselor not only does an excellent job of getting the American Indian children to school but also is good at raising their interest in school. The superintendent describes how the American Indian children's interest in school has increased over the years. "Our counselor has a two-step strategy. First, he gets the students involved in sports or band or some other extracurricular activity, which allow them to see that school events can be fun and exciting. Then, he seems to take this interest or excitement and move and/or expand it into the classroom, so that the students are interested in the classroom as well."

A final thought regarding the issue of awareness and sensitivity is made by some of the American Indian teachers in Clinton. They feel their presence does raise awareness and sensitivity, although they argue that more is needed. One teacher points this out by stating, "If all the American Indian teachers would make a more concerted effort, this would help increase consciousness and concern for our American Indian students. Still, even without being unified, we [American Indian teachers] have done a pretty good job of influencing the attitudes of other teachers and in building up their level of concern for American Indian students. But we would make more of an impact if there were more of us."

Finally, persons interviewed in both school districts believe that American Indian teachers, counselors, and minority teachers are important factors in the treatment of American Indian students because they are more sensitive to American Indian students. Some white teachers mention that American Indian teachers can relate and communicate better with American Indian students. For example, an American Indian student states, "The American

Indian teachers know and understand what we are going through at home and they understand our personality. We see them [American Indian teachers] at tribal functions, so they know us. But most of the white teachers do not know or understand us, although some try to." This corresponds with what the American Indian counselor in Clinton mentions about American Indian teachers as role models. She believes that American Indian teachers have more insight into the needs and problems of the American Indian students. In brief, after informal conversations with several American Indian students in Clinton, it is obvious that American Indian teachers are seen as role models.

Both superintendents state that American Indian teachers, or minority teachers in Watonga, are also important because there are less discipline problems with American Indian students in classes taught by American Indians. The superintendents argue that this is certainly, in part, a result of American Indian teachers being able to relate and communicate better and being more patient with American Indian students than are white teachers.

Another factor that is mentioned as influential in the treatment of American Indian students is cooperative learning. Cooperative learning is of particular interest because it involves the street-level bureaucratic behavior of teachers, which is seldom examined. Moreover, this factor is important because school districts can implement the use of cooperative learning more easily than they can hire American Indian teachers or counselors, based on the assumptions of limited budgets and small turnover in personnel. Superintendents and principals all note that a supply and demand problem is present with regard to American Indian teachers: There are very few American Indian teachers, and the demand for them is very high. One superintendent states, "We try to actively recruit American Indian teachers, but we cannot get any. The American Indians that go to college and get degrees are in such demand that they can go and do almost anything and few chose teacher education."

Cooperative Learning
Interviews in Clinton shed more light on cooperative learning than do interviews in Watonga. This is probably because the use of cooperative learning techniques in Watonga is not as widespread as it is in Clinton. The Clinton superintendent states that he feels confident in reporting that at least 80 percent of the teachers in the district use some form of cooperative learning. He goes on to suggest several reasons why cooperative learning is used: "I believe that our teaching staff has a higher concern for our students and their quality of education or their equal educational opportunities

than other teachers in other school districts. It is not just a concern, but it is also that we [the Clinton school district] have a high percentage of teachers with advanced degrees [beyond a bachelor's degree]. This training has helped to make our teachers more conscious of their behaviors and their teaching methods. Almost all our teachers are aware of the multiple benefits of cooperative learning. As a result of these different characteristics, I think that our teachers are more willing to try alternative methods of teaching, especially cooperative learning."

More important than determining why cooperative learning is used, is examining the reasons why cooperative learning is believed to be an important factor influencing Clinton's treatment of American Indians. For the most part, these reasons all focus around advantages outlined in previous research: increasing school integration by allowing for multiple-ability instruction and equal status of students, increasing student achievement, improving the social outcomes of schooling (such as intergroup relations and attitudes toward mainstreamed students), and producing positive effects on students' self-esteem. For example, one teacher spontaneously describes some of the benefits in the following matter: "Cooperative learning helps the students I come in contact with by making them feel good about themselves and good about learning in general. It gets the students, especially the American Indians, more involved and they end up participating a lot more than when I single them out. In this sense, I believe cooperative learning is very helpful because in the traditional classroom when questions are asked it always seems like the same students respond, while many of the others will not participate or pay attention and end up falling behind. Cooperative learning allows me to put lower ability students and higher ability students together, which enables all the students to experience success."

Several other teachers share the same attitudes and beliefs. One teacher emphasizes that he uses cooperative learning because it is the easiest way for slower students or lower ability students to improve. He believes that his higher ability students really seem to enjoy this as well. Another teacher sums up the reasons she uses cooperative learning by stating, "I have lots of diversity, in terms of students with different ethnic backgrounds, such as American Indians, and different abilities, in my classroom. Cooperative learning helps me to mix the class by ethnicity and ability. The students seem to respond very well to it and this has even cut down on some of my discipline problems."

When comparing the traditional competitive classroom to one with a cooperative environment, a few teachers refer to cooperative learning as "using the we concept, rather than the I concept. This [using cooperative learning] builds a sense of community, a sense of teamwork, where all the students get along and work together for the benefit of the whole. This helps the American Indian students in particular, but really all of the students, to learn invaluable social skills that they would be less likely to learn in a competitive classroom."

Moreover, as seen in these quotations, teachers believe their American Indian students perform better and are more involved in the class when cooperative learning techniques are employed. American Indian students in Clinton also believe this to be the case. All seven of the students say they prefer teachers who use cooperative learning, even if the teacher is not an American Indian.

Several other points about the use of cooperative learning in Clinton merit mentioning. First, the superintendent and each of the school principals state that they strongly encourage the use of cooperative learning. This is done in several ways. During job interviews they ask potential teachers about their familiarity with cooperative learning techniques and make a conscious decision to try to hire teachers familiar with cooperative learning techniques. Additionally, the principals, especially at the elementary and middle schools, encourage cooperative learning in their evaluation of teachers. One principal states, "If they [cooperative learning techniques] are not being used, then I ask the teacher why not and drop very obvious hints that they should be, not to mention the fact that the teacher's evaluations are scored lower. Teachers who are using cooperative learning are commended and almost always receive higher evaluations. I would say this is one reason why about 90 percent of our teachers use cooperative learning." This principal also points out that he makes regular classroom observations, usually once a week, if not more often.

The principals also encourage cooperative learning by establishing cooperative learning coordinators in each of their schools. These coordinators hold regular in-service workshops and teacher development meetings to discuss different aspects of cooperative learning. Finally, the schools, particularly the elementary and middle schools, are in the process of doing away with individual desks, which are being replaced with large tables that allow four to six students to sit around them. This is part of an attempt to facilitate and encourage the use of cooperative learning. Indeed, several teachers mention that the new tables make it difficult not to use cooperative learning. One teacher put it this way, "It is kind of hard to make lesson plans or structure lessons so that the students do not work and learn in cooperative learning teams, since they already sit in groups. In the long run, it really becomes easier to teach that way and more importantly when you consider the benefits that the students receive from cooperative learning, then it just makes more sense anyway."

Direct Observations

In addition to interviewing the personnel of the two Oklahoma school districts, classroom observations are also made. This includes observations at all of the schools within each school district, especially the elementary and middle schools. Observations are made in an attempt to move beyond interviewing, which is subjective in the sense that school district personnel's own words are used as a basis for indicating the importance of the particular factors in the school district's treatment of their American Indian students. Direct observation provides the opportunity to validate or invalidate the interviews, as well as findings from quantitative analysis. Principals of all the schools in each school district graciously granted permission to observe any of their teachers at any time. This permission allowed observations to be performed randomly throughout the different schools in each of the school districts without the teachers even knowing they might be observed.

The results of the observations seem to confirm the interviews, at least for the most part. Cooperative learning techniques are being used in almost all the classrooms in Clinton. Additionally, although they are also being used in Watonga, their use is not as widespread. This seems to follow the pattern established from the interviews. Furthermore, it seems that all students, not just the American Indians, are more involved and participatory in classes where cooperative learning is employed. In contrast, in the traditional competitive classroom, several students appeared to be daydreaming and less attentive. They did not respond to questions unless called upon, and even then some still did not respond.

American Indian students appear to be more outgoing, attentive, and engaging (asking and answering questions) in classes taught with American Indian teachers in the Clinton school district and with non–American Indian minority teachers in Watonga. Conversely, the American Indian students are more solemn and reserved in classes taught by non–American Indian teachers and non–minority teachers. This seems to correspond with the pattern established from the interviews.

Three Case Studies in Alabama

An Analysis of Important Factors Affecting the Treatment of American Indian Students

Table 7.3 shows the results of our coding scheme for the three Alabama school districts. In all three school districts—Jackson County, Lawrence

County, and DeKalb County—it appears that the single most important factor accounting for or at least influencing the school district's treatment of American Indian students is the presence of a well-established American Indian Education Program. In all three school districts, 100 percent of the respondents, either spontaneously or in response to a question, stated that the presence of an American Indian Education Program accounted for the school district's favorable treatment of American Indians. In fact, most interviewees spontaneously mentioned the American Indian Education Program as an important factor (81 percent in DeKalb County, 77 percent in Lawrence County, and 67 percent in Jackson County).

The only other spontaneously mentioned explanation of the school district's treatment of American Indian students is community attitudes or factors. Interviewees in Jackson County spontaneously mentioned the community 33 percent of the time, and 29 percent in DeKalb County and 24 percent in Lawrence County spontaneously mentioned the influence of the community. In total, a majority of interviewees in all three school districts either spontaneously or in response to a question mentioned the influence of the community as a major explanation for the school district's treatment of American Indian students (83 percent in Jackson County, 72 percent in DeKalb County, and 53 percent in Lawrence County).

Neither cooperative learning nor the presence of American Indian teachers is spontaneously mentioned by any of the respondents in the three school districts. This finding conflicts with the results of the case studies in our Oklahoma school districts, where the presence of American Indian teachers and the use of cooperative learning are the two most important explanatory factors. According to the interviewees in Alabama, cooperative learning appears to be more of a factor than the presence of American Indian teachers as an explanation for the school district's treatment of American Indian students. For instance, cooperative learning is mentioned as a factor in response to a question by 75 percent of the respondents in Jackson County, about half of the interviewees in DeKalb County, and 16 percent in Lawrence County. However, the presence of American Indian teachers is mentioned as a factor in response to a question by less than 17 percent of the respondents in all three school districts.

The finding suggesting the presence of American Indian teachers as not being an important factor in the school district's treatment of American Indian students is not surprising, if not misleading. Most, if not all, teachers in these three Alabama school districts who are considered to be American Indian are only part American Indian. Thus, American Indian teachers are not easily identifiable by the students.

Table 7.3
Possible Explanations for School District Treatment of American Indian Students: Jackson County, Lawrence County, and DeKalb County

Jackson County (N=100)

Mentioned	American Indian Teacher	Cooperative Learning	Community	American Indian Education Program
Spontaneously	0	0	33	67
In Response to a Question	17	75	50	33
Not a Factor	83	25	17	0

Lawrence County (N=99)

Mentioned	American Indian Teacher	Cooperative Learning	Community	American Indian Education Program
Spontaneously	0	0	24	77
In Response to a Question	8	16	29	23
Not a Factor	92	84	47	0

DeKalb County (N=98)

Mentioned	American Indian Teacher	Cooperative Learning	Community	American Indian Education Program
Spontaneously	0	0	29	81
In Response to a Question	14	46	43	19
Not a Factor	86	54	28	0

Note: Table reports percentages.

The same thing can also be said about American Indian students: They are not easily identifiable. This also partially explains why second generation discrimination toward American Indians is not prevalent in these three Alabama school districts. It is difficult to make any racial distinction between white students and American Indian students. This is not the case in Oklahoma, where often American Indian students are very easily identified.

Another method of determining explanations for the school district's treatment of its American Indian students is to assess the *importance* of each factor or explanation. This is accomplished by coding the apparent overall importance of the factor regardless of the number of times it is mentioned in the interview. The interviewees' comments relative to each factor are coded into two categories: The factor is likely to be either important or unimportant in the district's treatment of its American Indian students. The results appear in Table 7.4.

The patterns for each of the school districts are similar to the ones found in Table 7.3. For the Jackson County school district, the presence of the American Indian Education Program is considered important in every interview. The influence of the community is also considered to be an important factor for the school district's treatment as indicated by 74 percent of the interviewees. This is followed by cooperative learning, which is thought to be important by 31 percent of the persons being interviewed. Finally, none of the respondents believe the presence of American Indian teachers is an important factor. A similar pattern is found in the DeKalb County school district, with all respondents indicating that the presence of the American Indian Education Program as being important and 67 percent claiming community factors to be of importance. Only 13 percent of the interviewees believe cooperative learning to be of importance, and none of the respondents indicate American Indian teachers to be an important factor. In the Lawrence County school district, the only factor considered to be important is the American Indian Education Program, as is expressed by all the interviewees. The remaining factors are considered to be important by about one-third or less of the respondents (community, 34 percent; cooperative learning, 14 percent; and American Indian teachers, 0 percent).

Tables 7.3 and 7.4 establish the importance of the American Indian Education Program and, to some extent, community factors in the three school districts in Alabama. However, the tables do not show why these factors are "believed" to be important; thus a detailed discussion of each is merited.

Table 7.4
Importance of the Possible Explanations for School District
Treatment of American Indian Students: Jackson County, Lawrence County,
and DeKalb County

Jackson County (N=100)

Mentioned	American Indian Teacher	Cooperative Learning	Community	American Indian Education Program
Important	0	31	74	100
Unimportant	100	69	26	0

Lawrence County (N=99)

Mentioned	American Indian Teacher	Cooperative Learning	Community	American Indian Education Program
Important	0	14	34	100
Unimportant	100	86	66	0

DeKalb County (N=98)

Mentioned	American Indian Teacher	Cooperative Learning	Community	American Indian Education Program
Important	0	13	67	100
Unimportant	100	87	33	0

Note: Table reports percentages.

The American Indian Education Program

As discussed earlier in chapter 2, the American Indian Education Program is a federally supported program in which school districts are eligible for a certain amount of federal funds based on the number of identifiable American Indian students. School districts such as Jackson County, Lawrence County, and DeKalb County actively participate in this federal program by aggressively identifying eligible American Indian students and providing extra educational assistance to such students. In order for students to be eligible for the program, they must show that they possess at least one-thirty-second of American Indian ancestry and are a member of either a federally recognized Indian tribe or a state recognized Indian tribe.

The program is designed to provide several forms of educational assistance to identifiable American Indian students. Such assistance includes individual tutoring in math and reading along with preparation for SAT tests. American Indian students also participate in Indian culture and heritage classes and Indian arts and crafts classes. This extra assistance partially explains why American Indian students in these three school districts display higher graduation rates and are placed in gifted classes at a greater rate than other school districts. As one teacher noted, "The presence of an active American Indian Education Program is like having an extra dose of medicine."

Several administrators and teachers remarked that American Indian students feel that it is an honor and a privilege to participate in the program. In fact, one director of the American Indian Education Program stated, "Several non–American Indian students attempt to enroll in the program because of the benefits associated with the program." Many teachers and administrators in Alabama claim that the American Indian Education Program promotes a sense of higher self-esteem among American Indian students, increases understanding about American Indian culture and their heritage, and decreases behavior problems. These factors obviously contribute to equal educational attainment opportunities for American Indian students.

Community Influence

Many interviewees believe that the community is vital to reducing second generation discrimination of American Indian students. They claim that parents are actively involved in their children's education. One teacher remarked, "We have so many parents volunteering to help at school functions that we have waiting lists!" Another teacher noted, "The community is good about informing the school about Indian culture and events." Many teachers pointed out that skills that are culturally relevant to American Indian students are incorporated into the teaching at these schools. This kind of support is echoed in the sentiments of all the school personnel interviewed and helps account for the reason the community is viewed as an influence.

Several administrators and teachers also mentioned that a high degree of community support exists for American Indians and the American Indian Education Program. One teacher stated, "When future funding for the American Indian Education Program was in jeopardy, many parents attended school board meetings and contacted their congressmen in order to lobby against funding cutbacks and the possible elimination of the program."

Direct Observations

In addition to interviewing school district personnel of the three Alabama school districts, classroom observations are made in an attempt to validate or invalidate the interviews, as well as findings from earlier quantitative analyses. The interview process is somewhat subjective in the sense that school district personnel's own words are used as a basis for indicating the importance of the particular factors in the school district's treatment of their American Indian students. Principals of all schools in each school district graciously granted permission to observe teachers at any time.

The results of the observations seem to confirm the interviews. Cooperative learning techniques are used in several classrooms in Jackson County, in about half of the classrooms in Dekalb County, and in very few classrooms in Lawrence County. This follows the pattern established from the interviews. Where cooperative learning is used, it appears that all students are more involved and are more likely to engage in class discussions. In the traditional competitive classroom, students appear to be less attentive and less eager to engage in class discussions.

CONCLUSION AND IMPLICATIONS

This chapter describes the case studies of five school districts—two in Oklahoma and three in Alabama. The case studies were undertaken in an attempt to expand and enrich previous aggregate quantitative second generation discrimination analyses. Several major findings emerge from the case studies. First, and perhaps foremost, the case studies validate the importance of the case study methodology by suggesting that different factors are important in different school districts in mitigating the impact of second generation discrimination on American Indian students. After all, case studies have long been advocated as a method for better understanding the richness and dynamics of political phenomena. Case studies here point to the importance of American Indian teachers, American Indian counselors, and

African American and Hispanic teachers. The research posits that cooperative learning, as well as community support and attitudes, is important. Finally, another major factor affecting the treatment of American Indian students is the federal government sponsored American Indian Education Program and the aggressive response to this program on the part of Alabama school personnel. The case studies advance our better understanding of the dynamics of second generation discrimination beyond what we can learn from aggregate quantitative studies alone.

Second, the case studies reinforce the importance of minority teachers in public schools. Previous quantitative analyses discuss the importance of minority teachers, and the generalization now enjoys support at the micro, individual school district level. In addition to providing support to the importance of American Indian teachers, our case studies extend the second generation discrimination literature by highlighting some of the *reasons* that American Indian teachers, as well as counselors, are important. These reasons are that the American Indian teachers are role models for American Indian students, they raise sensitivity and awareness among teachers, and they are more sensitive to American Indian students. Thus, one strategy for mitigating second generation discrimination is simple—hire more minority teachers. Hiring more American Indian teachers is likely to decrease second generation discrimination among American Indian students.

Third, the case studies attempt to examine the behavior of teachers as street-level bureaucrats. The teaching methods instructors use affect second generation discrimination. Case study analyses find that cooperative learning techniques are important in the access of equal educational opportunities. Consequently, school districts should make better use of this pedagogical tool to reduce the second generation discrimination faced by all minority students, including American Indians. Furthermore, future aggregate quantitative studies on second generation discrimination should use the presence of cooperative learning techniques in a school as an important independent variable.

Fourth, the case studies emphasize the importance of American Indian programs and the response of school officials to such programs. The American Indian Education Program is the most important factor explaining the favorable treatment of American Indian students in the three Alabama school districts. This program produces many positive benefits for American Indian students. Such benefits include individual tutoring in math and reading courses, preparation for college entrance exams, increases in levels of self-esteem, and higher awareness of American Indian culture and heritage. These combined factors account for the positive academic performance of

American Indian students in the three Alabama school districts. Thus, one strategy for mitigating second generation discrimination among American Indian students is to implement an active and dynamic American Indian Education Program. The American Indian Education Programs in the three Alabama school districts seem to employ personnel that are diligent and display a genuine concern for American Indian students, which promotes the success of the programs.

Fifth, a finding emerging from the three Alabama school districts is that the presence of American Indian teachers is not perceived as an important factor accounting for the auspicious treatment of American Indian students, which contradicts the findings in Oklahoma and other previous studies. However, this is not to say that minority teacher presence is not an important factor in all school districts; it was, for instance, the most important factor in the two Oklahoma case studies. In Alabama, American Indian teachers and students simply are not as easily identifiable as they are in Oklahoma and other states such as New Mexico and Arizona.

NOTE

1. We will be happy to supply specific interview questionnaires upon request.

Chapter 8

Conclusion and Suggestions for Future Research

It has been more than twenty-five years since the U.S. Senate issued the Kennedy Report, which analyzed the education received by American Indian students. The report offered the following findings and conclusions: The national policies for educating American Indian students were failing by major proportions; there was low quality in virtually every aspect of the schooling available to American Indian children; the federal government's policy of "coercive assimilation" had "disastrous effects" on the education of American Indian children; and the American Indian students had not been "given educational opportunities anywhere near equal to that offered the great bulk of American children." Furthermore, it has been over twenty years since the Indian Education Act of 1972, the only piece of equal educational opportunity legislation specifically focused on American Indians, was enacted to address the educational inequities faced by American Indians.

The purpose of our research has been to evaluate the educational opportunities of American Indians. Similar to previous research regarding the educational opportunities of African Americans and Hispanics, our research demonstrates that equal educational opportunities for American Indians are still not a reality in all U.S. public schools. In this final chapter we (1) recapitulate major empirical findings emerging from the research; (2) highlight some of the major findings from the case studies and discuss possible strategies for mitigating second generation discrimination; and (3) offer some questions and suggestions for future research.

EMPIRICAL RESULTS

Today, most overt methods of segregation have been eliminated (but see McDonald 1989 on the overt methods of segregation used against American Indians). However, discrimination is still present in American public schools, only more subtle institutional methods of segregation are used to segregate minority and white children. Through the use of academic grouping and discipline, schools can limit interracial contact and deny minority students access to the best quality of education available in a school district. Our research shows that American Indian students are denied equal educational opportunities through the use of academic grouping as well as with discipline. Although these techniques are often simply viewed as good educational practices that are designed to benefit students, research demonstrates that the practices can facilitate second generation discrimination. The major empirical findings of our research support the discrimination argument.

First, American Indians are significantly overrepresented in lower-level academic groups, including EMR and LD classes, which negatively affect students. Additionally, American Indians are substantially underrepresented in higher-level academic groups, such as gifted classes, which have positive effects on students. Conversely, the exact opposite findings are revealed for white students; they are significantly overrepresented in higher-level academic groups and underrepresented in lower-level academic groups. For example, whites are overrepresented by almost 50 percent in the gifted classes and are about two and a half times more likely than American Indians to be placed in gifted classes. Furthermore, American Indian students are also far more likely to be disciplined through the use of school suspensions than are white students. Beyond our empirical findings, research from a multitude of educational scholars supports the propositions that assignments to lower-level academic groups and the unfair use of suspensions has detrimental effects on the students so assigned or disciplined.

Second, and once again similar to previous studies for African Americans and Hispanics, we determine that the measures of second generation discrimination for American Indian students are related (i.e., cluster together), whether they are analyzed using intercorrelation analysis or factor analysis. For example, all three academic grouping measures (EMR, LD, and gifted classes) have strong statistically significant correlations with suspensions. Similarly, in the factor analysis large suspension loadings are associated with a large number of EMR class placements and with the lack of gifted class placements for American Indian students. Multiple regression analyses reveal interrelationships among all the American Indian second generation discrimination indicators and show that academic grouping measures are determinants of suspensions. All these findings are consistent with the second generation discrimination hypothesis. The results form a pattern that could exist only if academic grouping has something in common with discipline.

Following these discoveries, which cumulatively mean that American Indian students do not receive equal educational opportunities, the research focus shifts toward ascertaining possible explanations for these occurrences. Viewing educational policy as a political process, our research employs a political model that examines several possible factors that might help explain the access of American Indian students to equal educational opportunities. These factors include American Indian representation, American Indian political resources, white poverty, and school district size.

Special attention is devoted to investigating the link between American Indian representation and American Indian student access to equal education. Teachers are extremely important as they make and implement school policies at the classroom level. They make initial judgments about students that directly or indirectly affect academic grouping and discipline. Indeed, the single most important and consistent variable in our theoretical model explaining second generation discrimination of American Indian students is the presence of American Indian teachers in our sample school districts. American Indian teachers produce policy outputs that benefit American Indian students and thus increase their access to equal educational opportunities. Specifically, we find negative relationships among American Indian teachers and the placement of American Indian students in EMR and LD classes, suspension rates, and the composite second generation discrimination factor. Conversely, positive relationships are identified between American Indian teachers and the placement of American Indian students in gifted classes and graduation rates. American Indian teachers translated passive representation in the school system into active representation for American Indian students.

Empirical research findings show that American Indian representation in administrative positions is the key to placing American Indians in teaching positions. Furthermore, when American Indians have political representation on school boards, American Indian representation in school administrative positions increases.

Our model posits that in addition to American Indian representation, American Indian resources influence equal educational opportunities for American Indian students. As we show in chapter 6, American Indian resources have only a modest impact on second generation discrimination. American Indian income is associated with higher gifted class placements and lower LD class placements for American Indian students. Data findings here are somewhat at odds with those reported for African American students, where African American political resources are found to be much more important (see Meier, Stewart, and England 1989). However, the impact of American Indian political resources is very similar to the impact of Hispanic political resources (see Meier and Stewart 1991). One possible reason for the difference may be the relatively low level of political resources possessed by American Indians, as well as Hispanics, compared to the levels possessed by African Americans.

White poverty has a significant impact on the suspension rates and the overall second generation discrimination factor for American Indian students. As predicted, these impacts are both negative. Increases in white poverty within the school district are associated with lower American Indian suspension ratios and overall lower levels of second generation discrimination. A modest relationship is found between white poverty and the American Indian gifted class ratio. As expected, an increase in white poverty within a school district results in somewhat more American Indian students being placed in gifted classes.

School district size has a significant impact on only one policy ratio, the suspension ratio. The impact is negative, meaning that an increase in the district size is associated with lower American Indian suspension ratios. Thus, it seems that the impact of district size on the overall level of second generation discrimination among American Indian students is only minimal.

In sum, our American Indian model of second generation discrimination, much like the Hispanic model, does not predict as well or explain as much variance as the African American model. Meier and Stewart (1991) argue that several reasons explain why this is the case for Hispanics. These reasons revolve around the fact that Hispanics possess lower levels of representation, education, and income in comparison to African Americans. A similar argument seems equally appropriate for American Indians, given that they have lower levels of representation, education, and income than either African Americans or Hispanics.

CASE STUDIES AND MITIGATING STRATEGIES

Our quantitative analyses identify American Indian teachers as the most consistent and influential factor impeding second generation discrimination among American Indian students. Previous research offers similar research findings for African Americans and Hispanics. Nevertheless, aggregate data findings do not explain why African American, Hispanic, and American

Indian teachers are so important. Additionally, quantitative data findings do not provide important information about teaching methods or other pedagogical tools teachers use. In contrast, our five case studies provide a better understanding of what goes on within schools.

Our case study analyses, through the use of interviews and classroom observations, establish the importance of the American Indian teacher and of the use of cooperative learning in the Clinton school district and the importance of the American Indian counselor and non–American Indian minority teachers in the Watonga school district. Consequently, the two case studies in Oklahoma support our findings from the quantitative analyses regarding the important impact American Indian teachers have in reducing second generation discrimination.

Besides supporting the importance of American Indian teachers, the two Oklahoma case studies present some of the reasons why American Indian teachers, as well as counselors, are influential in reducing the impact of second generation discrimination. The major reasons are that American Indian teachers are viewed as role models for American Indian students, they increase sensitivity and awareness among teachers, and they are more sensitive to American Indian students.

All five case studies find that the use of cooperative learning techniques is an important factor influencing the treatment of American Indian students. This positive effect results because cooperative learning increases school integration by allowing for multiple-ability instruction and equal status of students; cooperative learning increases student achievement; cooperative learning improves the social outcomes of schooling, such as intergroup relations and attitudes toward mainstreamed students; and cooperative learning produces positive effects on students' self-esteem. Additionally, teacher interviewees believe that all their minority students, including American Indians, participate more in class and perform better academically when cooperative learning techniques are employed in the classroom. Beyond the findings of our case studies regarding cooperative learning techniques, research from educational scholars supports the proposition that cooperative learning offers many advantages for minority students, especially American Indians (Brown 1980; Gordon and Boseker 1984; Reyhner 1992a, 1992b; Shutiva 1991; Slavin 1989; Slavin and Dickle 1981; Stokrocki 1992; Swisher 1990; Swisher and Deyhle 1989; Tonemah 1991).

In terms of strategies that may mitigate second generation discrimination, it seems that hiring more American Indian teachers should limit second generation discrimination among American Indian students. Furthermore, school districts should benefit from using cooperative learning teaching techniques, which appear to reduce the second generation discrimination American Indians experience.

Finally, the Alabama case studies offer three additional important findings. First, they support the notion that administrators and teachers as street-level bureaucrats possess high amounts of discretion in making and implementing policy. These case studies find that positive treatment of American Indian students is most affected by the American Indian Education Programs operating in the school districts. Local school personnel actively and aggressively implement this federally sponsored program to the immense benefit of local American Indian students. The point we make here is that the Alabama school officials could just as easily implement the program with little or no enthusiasm, or not at all.

Second, the Alabama case studies also illustrate the importance of community support on school board policies and activities. In all three districts the community is spontaneously mentioned as an important factor affecting the treatment of American Indian students in the district. Although we argue that community support is a necessary but not sufficient factor in the operation of a school system (fiscal resources and professional, caring school personnel are mandatory), the value of community support is practically immeasurable to district students.

The third lesson gained from the Alabama case studies is that race remains an important factor in American politics and, in our case, school politics. American Indians in Alabama are not easily identifiable and are sought out to secure additional school revenue. These American Indian students receive extra school services not because the law so mandates but because school personnel are happy and eager to provide such services. If the American Indian students in Alabama were easily identifiable, as they are in Oklahoma, New Mexico, and Arizona, would similar efforts be made to treat them so specially? We would hope so, but we remain a little skeptical.

Finally, one last benefit the case studies provide is to suggest some interesting questions for future research on second generation discrimination. These questions for future research are discussed below.

QUESTIONS FOR FUTURE RESEARCH

According to the 1994 U.S. Bureau of the Census population projections for the United States, minorities, including American Indians, African Americans, Hispanics, and Asians, represent between 67 and 90 percent of the population growth between now and the year 2010. Second generation discrimination issues and educational discrimination more broadly are likely to become even more salient and should warrant additional attention. The quantitative and qualitative components of our study raised a number of new research questions. These research questions are categorized into three different groups: those concentrating on explaining differences in the levels of second generation discrimination among minority groups, those generated from the case studies, and those dealing with the current political debates over educational policy.

Questions Concentrating on Explaining Differences in the Levels of Second Generation Discrimination among Minority Groups

Throughout this analysis, comparisons have been made among African Americans, Hispanics, and American Indians with respect to levels of second generation discrimination they encounter. Extreme caution must be taken in any direct comparisons between various quantitative studies, since sample sizes vary across the studies, different school districts are included in the samples, and second generation policy ratios are not measured for the same years. However, the level of second generation discrimination endured by American Indians appears to be less than that sustained by African Americans (based on the research by Meier, Stewart, and England 1989) and more than that encountered by Hispanics (based on the research by Meier and Stewart 1991). Although our analysis cannot explain the variation in the levels of second generation discrimination for these different minority groups, the literature offers some explanations.

One possible reason for different levels of second generation discrimination among American Indians, African Americans, and Hispanics involves a proposition from the power thesis of intergroup relations (see Blalock 1967; Giles 1975; Giles and Evans 1985, 1986). This proposition is that the proportion of a minority population in a community may influence group outcomes. That is, minorities can expect more favorable outcomes in communities where their populations are not salient enough to pose significant competition to the majority. Put differently, if the minority proportion of the overall community population is small, the minority is less likely to pose a tangible threat to the majority. In many respects this proposition is complementary to our argument that minority population is a political resource and that as it increases, political representation should also increase. Thus, as minority population (political power) increases, the threat to the white majority increases. Future research might investigate this issue by determining and testing a minority population "tipping point" into a model of second generation discrimination.

An alternative explanation for the differences found between minority groups may be related to Schneider and Ingram's (1993) contention that group "social construction" influences policy outcomes. They argue that how a group is socially constructed will affect the policy outcomes received in terms of benefits or burdens. For example, negatively constructed groups will be more likely to receive disproportionately negative outcomes, whereas positively constructed groups will be more likely to receive disproportionately more favorable outcomes. The variation in second generation discrimination across different minority groups may result from different social constructions. American Indian students are constructed more positively than African American students, whereas Hispanic students are constructed more positively than African American or American Indian students. It is important to note that the proportion of the minority's population will likely affect the development of its social construction. Therefore, this explanation is, at least somewhat, related to the first one.

Future research might examine the impact that social constructions of different minority groups have on second generation discrimination. This could be accomplished in several ways. First, determining the social construction of minority students could be achieved through the use of surveys. These surveys should focus on the attitudes, perceptions, and expectations that administrators, teachers, and counselors hold regarding different minority students. Students should also be surveyed in order to measure their attitudes toward how they are being stereotyped or socially constructed. An abundance of literature emphasizes that the expectations and attitudes of school personnel, especially teachers, can have a significant effect on student performance and equal educational opportunities. The point is also made that these expectations do not go unnoticed by students but, instead, become self-fulfilling prophecies. Social constructions may best be examined with studies including school districts that have significant levels of different minority students. Comparisons can be made among the minority groups and the impact of their respective social constructions.

Although the case studies performed for this analysis did not specifically address social constructions, many comments mentioned in the interviews provide a general sketch of the social constructions for American Indian students. These constructions included images of American Indian students as "quiet," "reserved," "laid-back," and "shy." These images and similar ones also enjoy widespread popularity in the literature on American Indian education. Although these constructions of American Indian students are not necessarily positive, they do seem somewhat more positive than the likely social constructions of African American students. Conventional wisdom suggests that minority students, but especially African Americans, may be unruly, rambunctious, and challenging of authority. These images are suggestive of negative constructions, especially in comparison to those for American Indians. If enough teachers have similar constructions for African American and American Indian students, then that may partially explain why the levels of second generation discrimination are lower for American Indian students than for African American students.

One final point regarding social constructions is that negative constructions regarding minorities as a whole may be a possible reason for second generation discrimination. For example, when teachers have negative constructions of minority students, they may watch these students more closely in an attempt to keep order in the classroom. This increased surveillance may lead a teacher to notice more disruptions from minorities. Consequently, the teacher may try to get the student out of the class and into a special education class or use more severe discipline. The idea is that the teacher does not want a spark to become a flame. Conversely, if teachers hold positive constructions of students, they may be less likely to watch them like a hawk and may also let some minor infractions go unpunished.

Additionally, with regard to school desegregation, it is important to point out that for many years both African Americans and American Indians had separate schools, whereas Hispanics were counted as "whites." Perhaps this may partially explain the lower levels of second generation discrimination faced by Hispanics. Another partial explanation for this may be that the tremendous amount of overrepresentation of Hispanics in bilingual education classes may cause their placement in other academic grouping areas, such as EMR or LD, to decrease. It has been suggested that bilingual education may be used as a relatively easy method for separating Hispanics and Anglos (Meier and Stewart 1991), whereas no such method exists in the case of African Americans or American Indians. Thus, if either of these two minority groups is to be separated from whites, other forms of academic grouping must be employed.

Another advantage American Indians and Hispanics have over African Americans, which may also be a factor accounting for part of the differences in the levels of second generation discrimination they face, is that they are less identifiable. Again this idea relates to the power thesis of intergroup relations (see Blalock 1967; Giles and Evans 1985, 1986). American Indians, especially those who physically resemble whites, can more easily be assimilated into white majority institutions than African Americans because they may be able to "pass" as white and are less likely than African Americans to be perceived as a threat. If this occurs, then African Americans may be more likely than American Indians or Hispanics to endure second generation discrimination. Findings emerging from the three Alabama case studies offer some support for this "light skin" thesis. Many times American Indians were difficult to identify and could pass as whites.

Finally, there are some other possible explanations why African Americans, Hispanics, and American Indians face differing levels of second generation discrimination, and these should be investigated in future research. These explanations require performing new research on several issues, including the following: the role and responsibility of the federal government in providing education for American Indian students, the importance of school sponsored clubs (such as multicultural clubs and American Indian clubs), the impact and pervasiveness of alternative teaching methods (such as cooperative learning), and the impact of parental involvement within school districts (such as the number of school volunteers or parent-teacher association members for each respective minority group). The three Alabama case studies support the importance of many of these factors.

Questions Generated from the Case Studies

Several future research questions emerge from our case studies. One of these questions revolves around the issue of whether minority teachers of one particular race or ethnicity provide benefits, in terms of less second generation discrimination, for minority students of a different race or ethnicity. The power theory of intergroup relations argued by Feagin (1980), Giles and Evans (1985, 1986), and Meier and Stewart (1991) would certainly not predict that minority teachers of one race or ethnicity would protect minority students of a different race or ethnicity. Instead, competition would be expected to exist among the different races and ethnic groups represented. Respective minority teachers would be expected to protect their respective minority students in a zero-sum game atmosphere. Conversely, the incorporation thesis argued by Browning, Marshall, and Tabb (1984) stresses cooperation of minority groups instead of competition. Therefore, future second generation discrimination research might test these theories.

An additional possible research question requires analyzing the impact of minority counselors. Generally, counselors do not hold teaching positions and have not been included in previous analyses of second generation discrimination. However, counselors possess some of the same types of bureaucratic discretion that teachers possess. Furthermore, counselors are involved in the overall assessment process of students. Thus, it would seem that if counselors have anywhere near the discretionary power that teachers possess, then they would be influential in second generation discrimination. Future research should include counselors in the analysis and should code their descriptive characteristics, especially their race or ethnicity, because these factors may affect second generation discrimination. Additionally, since teachers and counselors alike can be viewed as street-level bureaucrats, comparisons between them should be made in order to ascertain which is more influential in mitigating second generation discrimination.

Another suggestion for future research on second generation discrimination is that the street-level behavior of teachers merits more study. There is an abundance of literature that emphasizes the importance of teachers, although much of this literature overlooks the actual behavior or teaching methods of teachers. New studies should attempt to determine whether cooperative learning techniques or other pedagogical tools that school districts may employ have any effect on second generation discrimination. This would be useful in the sense that this information could be used to develop a knowledge base needed to suggest some possible strategies for mitigating second generation discrimination.

Finally, with regard to the case studies, more school districts need to be included for analysis. Case studies should be performed in the school districts that according to the quantitative results were the most likely to resegregate students but did not, or in the school districts that were least likely to resegregate students but did. Then comparisons could be made between the different school districts.

Questions Dealing with the Current Political Debates over Educational Policy

Other suggestions or research questions for future research concern some of the recent political debates regarding educational policy. The issue of school choice and the controversy surrounding it would make determining the impact of second generation discrimination on white enrollment (white flight) an important topic. It would be interesting to find out whether school districts with higher levels of second generation discrimination are able to limit their white enrollment losses over time. If school districts are able to limit white enrollment losses with the use of second generation discrimination techniques, then this may lessen the support for school choice. More importantly, future research should try to ascertain what implications second generation discrimination may have on the issue of school choice.

Although this research has not actually examined whether second generation discrimination is directly linked to academic performance in the classroom, unequal access to educational opportunities certainly implies a lower quality of education. Unfortunately, efforts to compare the quality of education that minority students, including American Indians, receive from different school districts is hampered by several factors. First, many test scores are not available from the school districts. Additionally, many times the tests are not comparable because different tests are given or the tests are given at different times during the school year. Moreover, in most school districts students placed in special education are excluded from taking the tests. Indeed, with the growing intense federal, state, and local pressure on school districts to raise their test scores, there is an added incentive to place students in special education (Artiles and Trent 1994; Gartner and Lipsky 1987). This becomes a method of raising the test scores of the school district. The problems previously mentioned in this area not withstanding, research in this area should be encouraged, because it would be a fruitful area for future research and would add tremendously to the second generation discrimination literature.

Appendix

ALABAMA
DeKalb County School District
Fort Payne City School District
Jackson County School District
Lawrence County School District

ALASKA
Anchorage School District
Bering Strait School District
Fairbanks North Star Borough School District
Juneau Borough School District
Kenai Peninsula Borough School District
Ketchikan Gateway Borough School District
Kodiak Island Borough School District
Lower Kuskokwin School District
Matanuska Susitna Borough School District

ARIZONA
Casa Grande District 82
Chinle Unit School District 24
Creighton School District 14
Flagstaff Unified District 1
Kayeata Unified District 27
Page Unified District 8
Sanders Unified District 18
Snowflake Unified District 5

ARIZONA (con't)
Tempe School District
Tuba City Unified District 15
Whiteriver Unified District 20
Window Rock Unified District 8

ARKANSAS
Gravette School District

CALIFORNIA
Anderson Union School District
Huntington Beach Union School District
Southern Humboldt Joint School District
Susanville School District

COLORADO
Montezuma-Cortez School District

IDAHO
Blackfoot School District 55

KANSAS
Arkansas City School District 470
Hiawatha School District 415

LOUISIANA
Sabine Parish School District
Terrebonne Parish School District

MAINE
Mashpee School District

MICHIGAN
Harbor Springs School District
Munising Public Schools
Rudyard Area Schools

MINNESOTA
Deer River School District
Minneapolis School District

MISSISSIPPI
Neshoba County Schools

MONTANA
Anaconda School District 10
East Helena School District 9
Great Falls Public Schools
Havre School District 16
Ronan School District 30

NEBRASKA
Scottsbluff Public Schools

NEVADA
Churchill County School District
Elko County School District
Lander County School District
Mineral County School District

NEW JERSEY
Ringwood Borough School District

NEW MEXICO
Aztec Municipal School District 2
Bernalillo Public Schools
Bloomfield Municipal Schools
Central Consolidated Schools 22
Farmington Municipal School District
Gallup-McKinley County Public Schools
Grants-Cibola County Schools
Los Lunas Public Schools
Pojoaque Valley School District
Taos Municipal School District
Tularosa Municipal Schools

NEW YORK
Center Moriches Schools

NORTH CAROLINA
Halifax County Schol District
Hoke County School District
Jackson County School District
Robeson County School District

NORTH DAKOTA
Belcourt 7 School District
Williston 1 School District

Bibliography

Agada, John, and Festus E. Obiakor. 1994. "The Politics of Education: Imperatives for African-American Males in the 21st Century." Paper presented at the Annual Conference of the National Association for Ethnic Studies, Kansas City, MO.

Algozzine, B., S. Christenson, and J. E. Ysseldyke. 1982. "Probabilities Associated with the Referral to Placement Process." *Teacher Education and Special Education* 5: 19-23.

Allen v. Merrell. 1956. 6 Utah 2d 32, 40.

Alozie, Nicholas O. 1996. "Race, Ethnicity, and Prosecutorial Discretionary Justice." Paper presented at the Annual Meeting of the Southwestern Political Science Conference, Houston, TX.

Anderson, James. 1984. *Public Policy Making* 3d. ed. New York: CBS College Publishing.

Anderson, P. L., M. E. Cronin, and J. H. Miller. 1986. "Referral Reasons for Learning Disabled Students." *Psychology in the Schools* 23: 388-95.

Armstrong, Liz Schevtchuk. 1991. "Report Attacks Enforcement of Ability-Grouping Practices." *Education Week* (May 1): 20.

Arnez, Nancy L. 1978. "Implementation of Desegregation as a Discriminatory Process." *Journal of Negro Education* 47: 28-45.

Artiles, Alfredo J., and Stanley C. Trent. 1994. "Overrepresentation of Minority Students in Special Education: A Continuing Debate." *Journal of Special Education* 27: 410-37.

Balch, R. W., and D. H. Kelly. 1974. "Reactions to Deviance in a Junior High School: Student's View of the Labeling Process." *Instructional Psychology* 1: 23-28.

Barlow, Donald L. 1984. "The Process of Native American Influence on the Education of Native American Children." *Journal of Thought* 19(3): 163-71.

Beare, Paul L. 1981. "Mainstreaming Approach for Behaviorally Disordered Secondary Students in a Rural School District." *Behavioral Disorders* 6: 209-18.

Beare, Paul L. 1986. "Programming for Behaviorally Disordered Native Americans." *Journal of American Indian Education* 25(3): 24-31.

Bickel, W. E. 1982. "Classifying Mentally Retarded Students: A Review of Placement Practices for Special Education," in Kirby A. Heller, Wayne H. Holtzman, and Samuel Messick (eds.), *Placing Children in Special Education*. Washington, D.C.: National Academy Press.

Bickel, William E., and Donna Diprima Bickel. 1986. "Effective Schools, Classrooms, and Instruction: Implications for Special Education." *Exceptional Children* 52: 489-500.

Blalock, Hubert M. 1967. *Toward a Theory of Minority-Group Relations*. New York: John Wiley and Sons.

Blumer, Herbert. 1958. "Race Prejudice as a Sense of Group Position?" *Pacific Sociological Review* 1: 3-7.

Bowles, S., and H. Gintis. 1976. *Schooling in Capitalist America*. New York: Basic Books.

Braddock II, Jomills Henry, and Marvin P. Dawkins. 1993. "Ability Grouping, Aspirations, and Attainment: Evidence from the National Educational Longitudinal Study of 1988." *Journal of Negro Education* 62: 324-36.

Braddock II, Jomills Henry, and Robert E. Slavin. 1993. "Why Ability Grouping Must End: Achieving Excellence and Equity in American Education." *Journal of Intergroup Relations* 20(1): 51-64.

Brantlinger, Ellen A. 1993. *The Politics of Social Class in Secondary School: Views of Affluent and Impoverished Youth*. New York: Teachers College Press.

Brescia, W., and J. C. Fortune. 1988. *Standardized Testing of American Indian Students—ERIC Digest*. ERIC Document Reproduction Service No. ED 296 813.

Bridges, Edwin. 1982. "Research on the School Administrator: The State of the Art." *Educational Administration Quarterly* 18(3): 12-33.

Brophy, William A., and Sophie D. Aberle. 1966. *The Indian America's Unfinished Business: Report of the Commission on the Rights, Liberties, and Responsibilities of the American Indian*. Norman, OK: University of Oklahoma Press.

Brown, A. 1980. "Cherokee Culture and School Achievement." *American Indian Culture and Research Journal* 4: 55-74.

Browning, Rufus P., Dale Rogers Marshall, and David H. Tabb. 1984. *Protest Is Not Enough*. Berkeley: University of California Press.

Bruch, C. 1975. "Assessment of Creativity in Culturally Different Children." *Gifted Child Quarterly* 19: 164-74.

Bullock, Charles S. , III, and Charles M. Lamb. 1984. *Implementation of Civil Rights Policy*. Monterry, CA: Brooks/Cole.

Bullock, Charles S., III, and Joseph Stewart, Jr. 1978. "Second Generation Discrimination in American Schools." *Policy Studies Journal* 7: 219-24.

Bullock, Charles S., III, and Joseph Stewart. 1979. "Incidence and Correlates of Second-Generation Discrimination," pp.115-29 in Marian L. Palley and Michael B. Preston (eds.), *Race, Sex, and Policy Problems*. Lexington, MA: Lexington Books.

Bureau of the Census, U.S. Department of Commerce. 1988. *We, The First Americans*. Washington D.C.: Government Printing Office.

Burlingame, Martin. 1986. "Using a Political Model to Examine Principals' Work." *Peabody Journal of Education* 63(1): 120-29.

Burtless, Gary. 1987. "Inequality in America: Where Do We Stand?" *The Brookings Review* 5: 9-16.

Carlberg, C., and K. Kavale. 1980. "The Efficacy of Special Versus Regular Class Placement for Exceptional Children: A Meta-Analysis." *Journal of Special Education* 14: 295-306.

Charles, Jim. 1987. "For the Sake of a Fed: The Misrepresentation of American Indians and Their Literature in High School: Literature Anthologies." *Journal of Ethnic Studies* 15(2):131-40.

Cherokee Nation v. Georgia. 1831. 30 U.S. 1.

Children's Defense Fund. 1974. *Children out of School in America*. Washington, D.C.: Children's Defense Fund of the Washington Research Project.

Children's Defense Fund. 1977. *The Elementary and Secondary School Civil Rights Survey: 'Bureaucratic Balderdash' or the Cornerstone of Civil Rights Compliance in Public Schools?* Washington, D.C.: Children's Defense Fund of the Washington Research Project.

Chinn, P. C., and S. Hughes. 1987. "Representation of Minority Students in Special Education Classes." *Remedial and Special Education* 8: 41-45.

Chubb, John E., and Terry M. Moe. 1990. *Politics, Markets, and America's Schools*. Washington, D.C.: The Brookings Institution.

Cibulka, James. 1991. "State Education Agencies and State-Local Relations: The Weak Links in Education Reform." Paper presented at the Annual Meeting of the American Educational Research Association, San Francisco, CA.

Cohen, D. K. 1982. "Policy and Organization: The Impact of State and Federal Educational Policy on School Governance." *Harvard Educational Review* 52: 474-99.

Cohen, Yinon, and Andrea Tyree. 1986. "Escape from Poverty: Determinants of Intergenerational Mobility of Sons and Daughters of the Poor." *Social Science Quarterly* 67: 803-13.

Cohn, Elchanan. 1979. *The Economics of Education*. Cambridge, MA: Ballinger Publishing.

Coleman, James S., Ernest Q. Campbell, Carol J. Hobson, James McPartland, Alexander B. Mood, Frederic D. Weinfeld, and Robert L. York. 1966. *Equality of Educational Opportunity.* Washington, D.C.: U.S. Government Printing Office.

Colodarci, Theodore. 1983. "High-School Dropout among Native Americans." *Journal of American Indian Education* 23(1): 15-22.

Connelly, Michael, and David E. Wright III. 1993. *Recent Developments in Volunteer Policy.* Weatherford, OK: C & H Research Consultants.

Coombs, M. 1970. "The Indian Student Is Not Low Man on the Totem Pole." *Journal of American Indian Education* 9(3): 1-9.

Croft, Carolyn. 1977. "The First American: Last in Education." *Journal of American Indian Education* 16(2): 15-19.

Crowson, Robert, and Van Cleve Morris. 1985. "Administrative Control in Large City Schools." *Educational Administration Quarterly* 21(4): 51-70.

Cummins, Jim. 1984. *Bilingualism and Special Education: Issues in Assessment and Pedagogy.* Avon, England: Multilingual Matters.

Cummins, Jim. 1986. "Empowering Minority Students: A Framework for Intervention." *Harvard Educational Review* 56(1): 18-36.

Cummins, Jim. 1989. *Empowering Minority Students.* Sacramento, CA: California Association for Bilingual Education.

Cummins, Jim. 1992. "The Empowerment of Indian Students," pp. 3-12 in Jon Reyhner (ed.), *Teaching American Indian Students.* Norman, OK: University of Oklahoma Press.

Davis, W. A., and Lorrie A. Shepard. 1983. "Specialist's Use of Test and Clinical Judgment in the Diagnosis of Learning Disabilities." *Learning Disabilities Quarterly* 19: 128-38.

Deere v. State. 1927. 22 F.2d 851 (N.D.N.Y.).

Deloria, Vine, Jr., and Clifford M. Lytle. 1983. *American Indians, American Justice.* Austin, TX: University of Texas Press.

Deno, E. 1970. "Special Education as Developmental Capital." *Exceptional Children* 37: 229-37.

Dodd, John M., and J. Ron Nelson. 1989. "Learning Disabled Adults: Implications for Tribal Colleges." *Journal of American Indian Education* 28(3): 31-38.

Downs, Anthony. 1967. *Inside Bureaucracy.* Boston: Little, Brown.

Duncan, Greg J. 1984. *Years of Poverty, Years of Plenty.* Ann Arbor: Institute for Social Research, University of Michigan.

Dunn, L. M. 1968. "Special Education for the Mildly Retarded: Is Much of It Justifiable? *Exceptional Children* 23: 5-21.

Dye, Thomas R., and James Renick. 1981. "Political Power and City Jobs: Determinants of Minority Employment." *Social Science Quarterly* 62: 475-86.

Easton, David. 1965. *A Systems Analysis of Political Life.* New York: Wiley.

Eberhard, David. 1989. "American Indian Education: A Study of Dropouts, 1980-1987." *Journal of American Indian Education* 29(1): 32-40.

Education Commission of the States. 1980. *Indian Education, Problems in Need of Resolution.* Denver, The Commission, Report No. 136.

Elder, D. 1983. "Ability Grouping and Students' Academic Self-Concepts: A Case-Study." *Elementary School Journal* 84: 149-61.

Engstrom, Richard L., and Charles J. Barrilleaux. 1991. "Native Americans and Cumulative Voting: The Sisseton-Wahpeton Sioux." *Social Science Quarterly* 72: 388-93.

Engstrom, Richard L., and Michael D. McDonald. 1981. "The Election of Blacks to City Councils." *American Political Science Review* 75: 344-54.

Eulau, Heinz, and Paul D. Karps. 1977. "The Puzzle of Representation: Specifying Components of Responsiveness." *Legislative Studies Quarterly* 2: 233-54.

Eulau, Heinz, John C. Wahlke, William Buchanan, and Leroy C. Ferguson. 1959. "The Role of the Representative: Some Empirical Observations on the Theory of Edmund Burke." *American Political Science Review* 53: 742-56.

Eyler, Janet, Valerie Cook, Rachel Thompkins, William Trent, and Leslie E. Ward. 1981. "Resegregation: Segregation within Desegregated Schools," pp. 210-329 in C. H. Rossell et al. (eds.), *Assessment of Current Knowledge about the Effectiveness of School Desegregation Strategies.* Nashville, TN: Institute of Public Policy Studies, Vanderbilt University.

Eyler, Janet, Valerie J. Cook, and Leslie E. Ward. 1983. "Resegregation: Segregation within Desegregated Schools," pp. 126-62 in Christine H. Rossell and Willis D. Hawley (eds.), *The Consequences of School Desegregation.* Philadelphia: Temple University Press.

Feagin, Joe R. 1980. "School Desegregation: A Political-Economic Perspective," pp. 25-50 in W. G. Stephan and J. R. Feagin (eds.), *School Desegregation: Past, Present and Future.* New York: Plenum Press.

Finley, Merrilee K. 1984. "Teachers and Tracking in a Comprehensive High School." *Sociology of Education* 57: 233-43.

Fitzgerald, Michael R., and David R. Morgan. 1977. "Changing Patterns of Urban School Desegregation." *American Politics Quarterly* 5: 437-63.

Florey, J., and N. Tafoya. 1988. *Identifying Gifted and Talented American Indian Students: An Overview. ERIC Digest.* Las Cruces, NM: ERIC Clearinghouse on Rural Education and Small Schools.

Fraga, Luis Ricardo, Kenneth J. Meier, and Robert E. England. 1986. "Hispanic Americans and Educational Policy: Limits to Equal Access." *Journal of Politics* 48: 850-76.

France-Kaatrude, A., and W. P. Smith. 1985. "Social Comparison, Task Motivation, and the Development of Self-Evaluative Standards in Children." *Developmental Psychology* 21: 1080-89.

Free, Lloyd A., and Hadley Cantril. 1967. *The Political Beliefs of Americans.* New Brunswick, N.J.: Rutgers University Press.

Friedrich, Robert J. 1982. "In Defense of Multiplicative Terms in Multiple Regression Equations." *American Journal of Political Science* 26: 797-833.

Froyen, Len A. 1993. *Classroom Management: The Reflective Teacher-Leader*. New York: Macmillan.

Gamoran, Adam. 1986. "Instructional and Institutional Effects of Ability Grouping." *Sociology of Education* 59(4): 185-98.

Gamoran, Adam. 1992. "Is Ability Grouping Equitable?" *Educational Leadership* 50(2): 11-17.

Gamoran, Adam, and Robert D. Mare. 1989. "Secondary School Tracking and Educational Inequality: Compensation, Reinforcement, or Neutrality?" *American Journal of Sociology* 94: 1146-83.

Gartner, Alan. 1986. "Disabling Help: Special Education at the Crossroads." *Exceptional Children* 53: 72-76.

Gartner, Alan, and Dorothy Kerzner Lipsky. 1987. "Beyond Special Education: Toward a Quality System for All Students." *Harvard Educational Review* 57: 367-95.

Giles, K. N. 1985. *Indian High School Dropout: A Perspective*. Milwaukee, WI: Midwest National Origin Desegregation Assistance Center, University of Wisconsin.

Giles, Michael W. 1975. "Black Concentration and School District Size as Predictors of School Segregation: The Impact of Federal Enforcement." *Sociology of Education* 48: 11-19.

Giles, Michael W., and Arthur S. Evans. 1985. "External Threat, Perceived Threat, and Group Identity." *Social Science Quarterly* 66: 50-66.

Giles, Michael W., and Arthur S. Evans. 1986. "The Power Approach to Intergroup Hostility." *Journal of Conflict Resolution* 30: 469-86.

Giles, Michael W., and Kaenan Hertz. 1994. "Racial Threat and Partisan Identification." *American Political Science Review* 88: 317-26.

Glass, Thomas E. 1986. "*Indian Oasis v. Warner*: A Case of Federal Supremacy in Public Education." *Journal of American Indian Education* 26(1):32-40.

Goggin, Malcolm L. 1986. "The 'Too Few Cases/Too Many Variables' Problem in Implementation Research." *Western Political Quarterly* 38: 328-47.

Goggin, Malcolm L., Ann O'M. Bowman, James P. Lester, and Laurence J. O'Toole, Jr. 1990. *Implementation Theory and Practice: Toward a Third Generation*. Glenview, IL: Scott, Foresman/Little, Brown Higher Education.

Gordon, Sandra L., and Barbara J. Boseker. 1984. "Enriching Education for Indian and Non-Indian Students." *Journal of Thought* 19(3): 143-48.

Gottlieb, Jay, Mark Alter, Barbara W. Gottlieb, and Jerry Wishner. 1994. "Special Education in Urban America: It's Not Justifiable for Many." *Journal of Special Education* 27: 453-65.

Grant, Linda, and James Rothenberg. 1986. "The Social Enhancement of Ability Differences: Teacher Student Interactions in First and Second-Grade Reading Groups." *Elementary School Journal* 87(September): 29-50.

Gross, Emma R. 1989. *Contemporary Federal Policy toward American Indians*. Westport, CT: Greenwood Press.

Guadalupe Organization v. Tempe Elementary School District No. 3. 1972. No. 71-435(D.. Arizona) (Consent decree).

Harrison v. Laveen. 1948. 67 Ariz. 337, 344.

Harry, B. 1992. *Cultural Diversity, Families, and the Special Education System: Communication for Empowerment*. New York: Teachers College Press.

Havighurst, Robert J. 1981. "Indian Education: Accomplishments of the Last Decade." *Phi Delta Kappan* 62: 5 (January): 329-31.

Hedge, D. M., D. C. Menzel, and G. H. Williams. 1988. "Regulatory Attitudes and Behavior: The Case of Surface Mining Regulation." *Western Political Quarterly* 41: 323-40.

Heidenheimer, Arnold J., Hugh Heclo, and Carolyn Teich Adams. 1990. *Comparative Public Policy: The Politics of Social Choice in America, Europe, and Japan*. 3d. ed. New York: St. Martin's Press.

Heller, Kirby A., Wayne H. Holtzman, and Samuel Messick, eds. 1982. *Placing Children in Special Education*. Washington, D.C.: National Academy Press.

Henig, Jeffrey R. 1985. *Public Policy and Federalism*. New York: St. Martin's Press.

Hergenreter v. Hayden. 1968. 295 F Supp. 251, Kan.

Hill, Norbert S., Jr. 1993. "Reclaiming American Indian Education," in Stanley Elam (ed.), *The State of the Nation's Public Schools: A Conference Report*. Bloomington, IN: Phi Delta Kappan.

Hillabrant, Walter, Mike Romano, David Stang, and Mike Charleston. 1992. "Native American Education at a Turning Point: Current Demographics and Trends," in Patricia Cahape and Craig B. Howley (eds.), *Indian Nations at Risk: Listening to the People. Summaries of Papers Commissioned by the Indian Nations at Risk Task Force of the U.S. Department of Education*. Charleston, WV: ERIC Clearinghouse on Rural Education and Small Schools.

Hirschfelder, Arlene, and Martha Kreipe de Montano. 1993. *The Native American Almanac: A Portrait of Native America Today*. New York: Prentice-Hall General Reference.

Hobson v. Hansen. 1967. 269 F Supp. 401.

Hochschild, Jennifer L. 1984. *The New American Dilemma: Liberal Democracy and School Desegregation*. New Haven, CT: Yale University Press.

Holliday, Bertha Garrett. 1985. "Differential Effects of Children's Self-Perceptions and Teachers' Perception on Black Children's Academic Achievement." *Journal of Negro Education* 54(winter): 71-81.

Hulburt, Graham, William Schulz, and Lyle Eide. 1985. "Using the Self-Directed Search with American Indian High School Students." *Journal of American Indian Education* 25(1):34-41.

Indian Appropriation Act of 1871, Act of March 3, 1987; 16 Stat. 544, 566; 25 U.S.C. 71.

Indian Nations at Risk Task Force. 1991. *Indian National at Risk: An Educational Strategy for Action: Final Report.* Washington, D.C.: U.S. Department of Education.

Indian Oasis et al. v. Warner et al. 1982. U.S. District Court, Tucson.

Jencks, Christopher, Marshall Smith, Henry Acland, Mary Jo Bane, David Cohen, Herbert Gintis, Barbara Heynes, and Stephan Michelson. 1972. *Inequality: A Reassessment of the Effect of Family and Schooling in America.* New York: Harper and Row.

Johnson, Marilyn J. 1992. "American Indians and Alaska Natives with Disabilities," in Patricia Cahape and Craig B. Howley (eds.), *Indian Nations at Risk: Listening to the People. Summaries of Papers Commissioned by the Indian Nations at Risk Task Force of the U.S. Department of Education.* Charleston, WV: ERIC Clearinghouse on Rural Education and Small Schools.

Johnson, D. W., R. T. Johnson, E. J. Holubec, and P. Roy. 1984. *Circles of Learning.* Alexandria, VA: Association for Supervision and Curriculum Development.

Jones, Effie H. and Xenia P. Montenegro. 1982. "Toward an Equitable Representation of Minorities in School Administration." Arlington, VA: American Association of School Administrators.

Jones, Reginald L., ed. 1976. *Mainstreaming and the Minority Child.* Reston, VA: Council for Exceptional Children.

Jordan, Will J., Julia Lava, and James M. McPartland. 1994. *Exploring the Complexity of Early Dropout Causal Structures.* Baltimore, MD: Center for Research on Effective Schooling for Disadvantaged Students, Johns Hopkins University.

Joshi, Sneha M., and V. D. Thomas. 1991. "Innovations in Teacher Education—The Indian Context." *Action in Teacher Education* 13(3): 11-15.

Kaeser, Susan C. 1979. "Suspensions in School Discipline." *Education and Urban Sociology* ll: 465-86.

Kaestle, Carl F., and Marshall S. Smith. 1982. "The Federal Role in Elementary and Secondary Education, 1940-1980. *Harvard Educational Review* 52: 384-408.

Kerr, Brinck, and Kenneth R. Mladenka. 1994. "Does Politics Matter? A Time-Series Analysis of Minority Employment Patterns." *American Journal of Political Science* 38: 918-43.

King, Gary, Robert O. Keohane, and Sidney Verba. 1994. *Designing Social Inquiry: Scientific Inference in Qualitative Research.* Princeton, NJ: Princeton University Press.

Kingdon, John W. 1989. *Congressmen's Voting Decisions.* 3d ed. Ann Arbor: University of Michigan Press.

Kingsley, J. Donald. 1944. *Representative Bureaucracy.* Yellow Springs, OH: Antioch Press.

Kirksey, Jason F., and David E. Wright III. 1992. "Black Women in State Legislatures: The View from Oklahoma." *Oklahoma Politics* 1: 67-79.

Knutson, Kari A., and Sherri N. McCarthy-Tucker. 1993. "Gifted Education for Native American Students: A State of Affairs." Roundtable presentation at the Meeting of the American Educational Research Association, Atlanta, GA.

Korinek, Lori. 1987. "Questioning Teacher Feedback Practices: What Goes on in Special Classes?" *Diagnostique* 12(2): 93-102.

Kozol, Jonathan. 1985. *Illiterate America*. New York: New American Library.

Kulik, James A., and Chen-Lin C. Kulik. 1982. "Effects of Ability Grouping on Secondary School Students: A Meta-Analysis of Evaluation Findings." *American Educational Research Journal* 19: 415-28.

Kulik, James A., and Chen-Lin C. Kulik. 1984. "Effects of Accelerated Instruction on Students." *Review of Educational Research* 54: 409-25.

Kulik, James A., and Chen-Lin C. Kulik. 1987. "Effects of Ability Grouping on Student Achievement." *Equity and Excellence* 23(spring): 22-30.

Lasswell, Harold. D. 1936. *Politics: Who Gets What, When, How?* New York: McGraw-Hill.

Latham, Glenn I. 1984. "Fifteen Most Common Needs of Indian Education." Paper presented at the National Indian Child Conference, Albuquerque, NM.

Latham, Glenn I. 1985. "The Educational Status of Federally Recognized Indian Students." *Journal of American Indian Education* 25(1): 25-33.

Latham, Glenn I. 1989. "Thirteen Most Common Needs of American Education in BIA Schools." *Journal of American Indian Education* 29(1): 1-11.

Lee, Valerie E., and Anthony S. Bryk. 1988. "Curriculum Tracking as Meditating the Social Distribution of High School Achievement." *Sociology of Education* 61: 78-95.

Levin, Betsy, and Phillip Moise. 1975. "Litigation in the Seventies and the Use of Social Science Evidence: An Annotated Guide." *Law and Contemporary Problems* 39: 50-133.

Levin, Henry M. 1975. "Education, Life Chances, and the Courts: The Role of Social Science Evidence." *Law and Contemporary Problems* 39: 217-39.

Levitan, David M. 1946. "The Responsibility of Administrative Officials in a Democratic Society." *Political Science Quarterly* 61(December): 562-98.

Lineberry, Robert L. 1978. "Reform, Representation, and Policy." *Social Science Quarterly* 59: 173-77.

Lineberry, Robert L., and Edmund P. Fowler. 1967. "Reformism and Public Policies in American Cities." *American Political Science Review* 61: 701-16.

Lipsky, Michael. 1980. *Street Level Bureaucracy*. New York: Russell Sage Foundation.

Little Thunder v. South Dakota, 518 F.2d 1253 (8th Cir. 1975).

Long, Norton E. 1952. "Bureaucracy and Constitutionalism." *American Political Science Review* 46(September): 808-18.

Lovrich, Nicholas P. 1974. "Differing Priorities in an Urban Electorate." *Social Science Quarterly* 55: 704-17.

Lovrich, Nicholas P., and G. Thomas Taylor. 1976. "Neighborhood Evaluation of Local Government Services: A Citizen Survey Approach." *Urban Affairs Quarterly* 12: 197-222.

Lowi, Theodore. 1969. *The End of Liberalism*. New York: Norton.

Lutz, Frank W., and Donald A. Barlow. 1980. "The Process of Native American Influence on the Education of Native American Children." Paper presented at the Annual Meeting of the American Educational Research Association, Boston, MA.

Lutz, Frank W., and Donald A. Barlow. 1981. "School Boards and the Process of Native American Influence on the Education of Native American Children." *Journal of Educational Equity and Leadership* 1(2): 90-97.

Lynch, Patrick D., and Mike Charleston. 1990. "The Emergence of American Indian Leadership in Education." *Journal of American Indian Education* 29(2): 1-10.

MacMillan, D. L. 1988. "Issues in Mild Mental Retardation." *Education and Training in Mental Retardation* 23: 273-84.

Madden, Nancy A., and Robert L. Slavin. 1982. *Count Me In: Academic Achievement and Social Outcomes of Mainstreaming Students with Mild Academic Handicaps*. Baltimore: Johns Hopkins University Press.

Maker, J. 1983. "Quality Education for Gifted Minority Students." *Journal for the Education of the Gifted* 6(3): 140-53.

Mann, Dale. 1976. *The Politics of Administrative Representation*. Lexington, MA: Lexington Books.

Mansfield, Wendy, and Elizabeth Farris. 1992. *Office for Civil Rights Survey Redesign: A Feasibility Survey*. Rockville, MD: Westat.

Marotto, R. A. 1986. "'Posin' to Be Chosen': An Ethnographic Study of In-School Truancy," pp.193-211 in D. M. Fetterman and M. A. Pitman (eds.), *Educational Evaluation: Ethnography in Theory, Practice, and Politics*. Beverly Hills: Sage.

Masten, W. G. 1981. *Approaches to Identification of Gifted Minority Students*. Jackson, MS: Mississippi State University (ERIC Reproduction Document Service No. ED 234 578).

McCool, Daniel. 1985. "Indian Voting," pp. 105-34 in Vine Deloria, Jr. (ed.), *American Indian Policy in the Twentieth Century*. Norman, OK: University of Oklahoma Press.

McCoy, Melanie. 1992. "The Impact of Oklahoma Indian Tribes on the Political Agenda of the U.S. Government." *Oklahoma Politics* 1: 49-66.

McDonald, Dennis. 1989. "The Politics of Control: From No Power to Local Power?" *Education Week* (Special Report, August 2): 9-11.

McFadden, Anna C., George E. Marsh II, Barrie Jo Price, and Yunhan Hwang. 1992. "A Study of Race and Gender Bias in the Punishment of School Children." *Education and Treatment of Children* 15(2): 140-46.

McIntyre, L. L. 1990. "Teacher Standards and Gender: Factors in Special Education Referral?" *Journal of Educational Research* 83: 166-72.

McLaren, P. L. 1987. "On Ideology and Education: Critical Pedagogy and the Politics of Empowerment." *Social Text* 7: 153-86.

McQuiston, John M., and Rodney L. Brod. 1984. "Structural and Cultural Conflict in American Indian Education." *Journal of Thought* 19(3):48-58.

Mecca, Frank. 1992. "Neither Equitable nor Excellent: The Effects of Tracking on Minority Students," pp. 47-63 in *Securing Our Future: The Importance of Quality Education for Minorities. Policy Research Project Report Number 96.* Austin, TX: Lyndon B. Johnson of Public Affairs.

Meier, Kenneth J. 1975. "Representative Bureaucracy: An Empirical Analysis." *American Political Science Review* 69: 526-42.

Meier, Kenneth J. 1987. *Politics and the Bureaucracy: Policymaking in the Fourth Branch of Government.* 2d. ed. Monterey, CA: Brooks/Cole Publishing Company.

Meier, Kenneth J. 1993. "Latinos and Representative Bureaucracy: Testing the Thompson and Henderson Hypotheses." *Journal of Public Administration Research and Theory* 3(4): 393-414.

Meier, Kenneth J., and Robert E. England. 1984. "Black Representation and Educational Policy: Are They Related?" *American Political Science Review* 78: 392-403.

Meier, Kenneth J., and Lloyd G. Nigro. 1976. "Representative Bureaucracy and Policy Preferences." *Public Administration Review* 36(July/August): 458-70.

Meier, Kenneth J., and Joseph Stewart, Jr. 1991. *The Politics of Hispanic Education.* Albany, NY: State University Press.

Meier, Kenneth J., Joseph Stewart, Jr., and Robert E. England. 1989. *Race, Class, and Education: The Politics of Second-Generation Discrimination.* Madison, WI: University of Wisconsin Press.

Meier, Kenneth J., Joseph Stewart, Jr., and Robert E. England. 1991. "The Politics of Bureaucratic Discretion: Educational Access as an Urban Service." *American Journal of Political Science* 35: 155-77.

Mercer, Cecil D. 1987. *Students with Learning Disabilities.* 3d. ed. Columbus, OH: Merrill Publishing Company.

Mercer, Jane R. 1973. *Labeling the Mentally Retarded.* Berkeley: University of California Press.

Mercer, Mary M. 1982. "Reassessing the Large Number of Black Children in Special Education Classes: A Challenge for the 80's." *Negro Educational Review* 33(1): 28-33.

Meriam, Lewis. 1928. *The Problem of Indian Administration.* Baltimore, MD: Johns Hopkins University.

Messick, Samuel. 1984. "Assessment in Context: Appraising Student Performance in Relation to Instructional Quality." *Educational Researcher* 13(March): 3-8.

Metz, Mary Haywood. 1978. *Classrooms and Corridors: The Crisis of Authority in Desegregated Secondary Schools.* Berkeley, CA: University of California Press.

Meyer, D. E. 1972. "We Continue to Massacre the Education of the American Indian." *Journal of American Indian Education* 11(2): 18-25.

Middletown School Committee v. Board of Regents for Education of Rhode Island. 1977. 439 F. Supp. 1122 (D.R.L.).

Mills, Carol J., and William G. Durden. 1992. "Cooperative Learning and Ability Grouping: An Issue of Choice." *The Gifted Child Quarterly* 36: 11-16.

Mladenka, Kenneth R. 1980. "The Urban Bureaucracy and the Chicago Political Machine." *American Political Science Review* 74: 991-98.

Mladenka, Kenneth R. 1989a. "Blacks and Hispanics in Urban Politics." *American Political Science Review* 83: 165-92.

Mladenka, Kenneth R. 1989b. "Barriers to Hispanic Employment Success in 1,200 Cities." *Social Science Quarterly* 70: 391-407.

Moe, Terry M. 1982. "Regulatory Performance and Presidential Administration." *American Journal of Political Science* 26: 531-43.

Monk, David H. 1992. "Education Productivity Research: An Update and Assessment of Its Role in Education Finance Reform." *Educational Evaluation and Policy Analysis* 14: 307-32.

Montoya v. Bolack. 1962. 70 N.M. 196.

Mosher, Frederick C. 1968. *Democracy and the Public Service.* New York: Oxford University Press.

Mosher, Frederick C. 1982. *Democracy and the Public Service* 2d. ed. New York: Oxford University Press.

Murray, Charles. 1984. *Losing Ground: American Social Policy, 1950-1980.* New York: Basic Books.

National Advisory Council on Indian Education. 1990. *Toward the Year 2000: Listening to the Voice of Native America, 17th Annual Report to the U.S. Congress.* Washington, D.C.: The Council.

Newell, J., and M. C. Tyon. 1989. "The Silent Minority: Working with Traditional American Indian Students in Cooperative Education Programs." *Journal of Cooperative Education* 25: 79-87.

Noley, Grayson. 1992. "Native and Non-Native Teachers and Administrators for Elementary and Secondary Schools Serving American Indian and Alaska Native Students." in Patricia Cahape and Craig B. Howley (eds.), *Indian Nations at Risk: Listening to the People. Summaries of Papers Commissioned by the Indian Nations at Risk Task Force of the U.S. Department of Education.* Charleston, WV: ERIC Clearinghouse on Rural Education and Small Schools.

O'Brien, Eileen M. 1990a. "The Demise of Native American Education, Part I." *Black Issues in Higher Education* 7(1): 15-22.

O'Brien, Eileen M. 1990b. "The Demise of Native American Education, Part II. A Foot in Each World: American Indians Striving to Succeed in Higher Education." *Black Issues in Higher Education* 7(2): 27-31.

O'Connell, J. C. 1987. *A Study of the Special Problems and Needs of American Indians with Handicaps Both on and off the Reservation.* Volume 1. Flagstaff, AZ: Northern Arizona University Native American Research and Training Center and Tucson, AZ: University of Arizona Native American Research and Training Center.

Oakes, Jeannie. 1985. *Keeping Track: How Schools Structure Inequality.* New Haven, CT: Yale University Press

Oakes, Jeannie. 1988. "Tracking: Can Schools Take a Different Route?" *National Education Association* 6: 41-47.

Ogbu, John U. 1986. "Structural Constraints in School Desegregation," pp. 21-45 in J. Prager, D. Longshore, and M. Seeman (eds.), *School Desegregation Research: New Directions in Situational Analysis.* New York: Academic Press.

Ogbu, John U. 1978. *Minority Education and Caste: The American System in Cross-Cultural Perspective.* New York: Academic Press.

Oklahoma Department of Libraries. 1991. *Directory of Oklahoma: State Almanac, 1991-1992.* Oklahoma City, OK: Oklahoma Department of Libraries.

Olivas, Michael A. 1983. "Research and Theory on Hispanic Education: Students, Finance, and Governance." *Aztlan* 14 (spring): 111-46.

Ortiz, Alfonso A., and J. R. Yates. 1983. "Incidence of Exceptionality among Hispanics: Implications for Manpower Planning." *NABE Journal* 7:41-54.

Padilla, E. R., and G. E. Wyatt. 1983. "The Effects of Intelligence and Achievement Testing on Minority Group Children," pp. 417-37 in G. J. Powell (ed.), *The Psychosocial Development of Minority Group Children.* New York: Brunner/Mazel.

Pavel, D. Michael, Thomas R. Curtin, Judy M. Thorne, Bruce Christenson, Blair A. Rudes, and Summer D. Whitener. 1995. *Characteristics of American Indian and Alaska Native Education.* Washington, D.C.: U.S. Department of Education, Office of Educational Research and Improvement, National Center for Education Statistics.

Pertusati, Linda. 1988. "Beyond Segregation or Integration: A Case Study from Effective Native American Education." *Journal of American Indian Education* 27(2): 10-20.

Pettigrew, Thomas F. 1991. "Normative Theory in Intergroup Relations: Explaining Both Harmony and Conflict." *Psychology and Developing Societies* 3: 3-16.

Pettigrew, Thomas F. 1994. "Prejudice and Discrimination on the College Campus." *Higher Education Extension Service Review* 6(1): 1-9.

Pitkin, Hanna F. 1967. *The Concept of Representation.* Berkeley: University of California Press.

Plessy v. Ferguson. 1896. 163 U.S. 537.

Polinard, J. L., Robert D. Wrinkle, and Tomas Longoria. 1990. "Education and Governance: Representational Links to Second Generation Discrimination." *Western Political Quarterly* 43: 631-46.

Porter v. Hall. 1928. 34 Ariz. 308, 321.

Prewitt, Kenneth. 1970. "Political Ambitions, Volunteerism, and Electoral Accountability." *American Political Science Review* 64: 5-17.

Prince v. Board of Education. 1975. 88 N.M. 548, 543 P.2d 1176.

Prucha, Francis Paul. 1984. *The Great Father: The United States Government and the American Indians* Volumes 1 & 2. Lincoln, NE: University of Nebraska Press.

Putnam, Jo Anne W. 1993. *Cooperative Learning and Strategies for Inclusion: Celebrating Diversity in the Classroom.* Baltimore, MD: Paul H. Brookes Publishing Company.

Radin, Norma. 1988. "Alternatives to Suspension and Corporal Punishment." *Urban Education* 22(January): 476-95.

Ramirez, B. A., and M. J. Johnson. 1988. "American Indian Exceptional Children: Improving Practices and Policy." pp. 76-85 in A. Ortiz and B. A. Ramirez (eds.), *Schools and the Culturally Diverse Exceptional Student: Promising Practices and Future Directions.* Reston, VA: Council for Exceptional Children.

Redford, Emmette S. 1969. *Democracy in the Administrative State.* New York: Oxford University Press.

Reschly, Daniel J. 1978. "WISC-R Factor Structures among Anglos, Blacks, Chicanos, and Native American Papagos." *Journal of Consulting and Clinical Psychology* 46: 417-22.

Reschly, Daniel J. 1981. "Psychological Testing in Educational Classification and Placement." *American Psychologist* 36(10): 1094-1102.

Reschly, Daniel J. 1987. "Learning Characteristics of Mildly Handicapped Students: Implications for Classification, Placement, and Programming," pp. 35-58 in M. C. Wang, M. C. Reynolds, and H. J. Walberg (eds.), *Handbook of Special Education.* Oxford, England: Pergamon.

Reschly, Daniel J., Richard Kicklighter, and Patrick McKee. 1988. "Recent Placement Litigation Part III: Analysis of Differences in Larry P., Marshall and S-1 and Implications for Future Practices." *School Psychology Review* 17(1): 39-50.

Reyhner, Jon. 1992a. "American Indians out of School: A Review of School-Based Causes and Solutions." *Journal of American Indian Education* 31(3): 37-56.

Reyhner, Jon. 1992b. *Teaching American Indian Students.* Norman, OK: University of Oklahoma Press.

Rhodes, R. W. 1989. "Standardized Testing of Minority Students: Navajo and Hopi Examples." *Journal of Navajo Education* 6(2): 29-35.

Robbins, Rockey. 1991. "American Indian Gifted and Talented Students: Their Problems and Proposed Solutions." *Journal of American Indian Education* 31(1): 15-24.

Robinson, Theodore P., and Thomas R. Dye. 1978. "Reformism and Black Representation on City Councils." *Social Science Quarterly* 59: 133-41.

Robinson, Theodore P., and Robert E. England. 1981. "Black Representation on Central City School Boards Revisited." *Social Science Quarterly* 62: 495-502.

Rodgers, Harrell R., and Charles S. Bullock. 1972. *Law and Social Change*. New York: McGraw-Hill.

Rosenbaum, James E. 1976. *Making Inequality: The Hidden Curriculum of High School Tracking*. New York: John Wiley.

Rourke, Francis E. 1984. *Bureaucracy, Politics and Public Policy*. 3d. ed. Boston: Little, Brown.

Ryan, Frank Anthony. 1982. "The Federal Role in American Indian Education." *Harvard Educational Review* 52: 423-30.

Rynders, John E., Stuart J. Schleien, Luanna H. Meyer, Terri L. Vandercook, Theresa Mustonen, Josefina S. Colond, and Kathleen Olson. 1993. "Improving Integration Outcomes for Children with and without Severe Disabilities through Cooperatively Structured Recreation Activities: A Synthesis of Research." *Journal of Special Education* 26(4): 386-407.

Saltzstein, Grace Hall. 1979. "Representative Bureaucracy and Bureaucratic Responsibility." *Administration and Society* 10(February): 465-75.

Saltzstein, Grace Hall. 1983. "Personnel Directors and Female Employment Representation." *Social Science Quarterly* 64: 734-46.

Santo, Beverly. 1990. "Bicultural Education among Indian Americans." Proceedings of the 4th National Forum of the Association of Independent Liberal Arts Colleges for Teacher Education, Milwaukee, WI.

Schafer, Walker E., and Carol Olexa. 1971. *Tracking and Opportunity: The Locking out Process and Beyond*. Scranton, PA: Chandler.

Schermerhorn, R. A. 1956. "Power as a Primary Concept in the Study of Minorities." *Social Forces* 35: 53-56.

Schneider, A., and H. Ingram. 1993. "Social Constructions and Target Populations: Implications for Politics and Policy." *American Political Science Review* 87: 334-47.

Schultz, Theodore. 1961. "Investment in Human Capital." *American Economic Review* 51: 1-17.

Schultz, Theodore. 1963. *The Economic Value of Education*. New York: Columbia University Press.

Schunk, D. H. 1987. "Peer Models and Children's Behavioral Change." *Review of Educational Research* 57(2): 149-74.

Schwartz, Louis. 1990. "Special Education Tracks of Inequality." Paper presented at the Council for Exceptional Children Symposia on Culturally Diverse Exceptional Children, Albuquerque, NM.

Schwille, John, Andrew Porter, and Michael Gant. 1980. "Content Decision-Making and the Politics of Education." *Educational Administration Quarterly* 16: 21-40.

Seminole Nation v. United States. 1942. 316 U.S. 286.

Serrano v. Priest. 1971. 96 Cal.Rptr 601, 487 P2d 1241.

Sharpes, Donald K. 1979. "Federal Education for the American Indian." *Journal of American Indian Education* 19(1):19-22.

Shepard, Lorrie A. 1987. "The New Push for Excellence: Widening the Schism between Regular and Special Education." *Exceptional Children* 53: 327-29.

Shepard, Lorrie A., L. A. Smith, and C. P. Vojir. 1983. "Characteristics of Pupils Identified as Learning Disabled." *Journal of Special Education* 16: 73-85.

Shirley v. Superior Court. 1973. 109 Ariz. 510.

Shutiva, Charmaine L. 1991. "Creativity Differences between Reservation and Urban American Indians." *Journal of American Indian Education* 31(1): 33-52.

Singer, Judith D., and John A. Bulter. 1987. "The Education for All Handicapped Children Act: Schools as Agents for Social Reform." *Harvard Education Review* 57 125-52.

Singer, Judith D., John A. Bulter, Judith S. Palfrey, and Deborah K. Walker. 1986. "Characteristics of Special Education Placement: Findings from Probability Samples in Five Metropolitan School Districts." *Journal of Special Education* 20: 319-37.

Sires, Carolyn, and Sandra Tonnesen. 1993. "Special Education: A Challenge for Principals." *NASSP Bulletin* 77(February): 8-11.

Slavin, Robert E. 1980. "Cooperative Learning in Teams: State of the Art." *Educational Psychologist* 15 (summer): 93-111.

Slavin, Robert E. 1981. "Cooperative Learning and Desegregation." pp. 244-55 in Willis D. Hawley (ed.), *Effective School Desegregation: Equity, Quality, and Feasibility.* Beverly Hills, CA.: Sage.

Slavin, Robert E. 1982. *Cooperative Learning.* New York: Longman.

Slavin, Robert E. 1986. *Using Student Team Learning* 3d ed. Baltimore, MD: Johns Hopkins University Press.

Slavin, Robert L. 1987. "Ability Grouping and Student Achievement in Elementary Schools: A Best Evidence Synthesis." *Review of Education Research* 57: 293-336.

Slavin, Robert E. 1988. *Student Team Learning: An Overview and Practical Guide.* 2d. ed. Washington, D.C.: National Education Association.

Slavin, Robert E. 1988. "Synthesis of Research in Elementary and Secondary Schools." *Educational Leadership* 46(1): 67-77.

Slavin, Robert E. 1989. "Research on Cooperative Learning: Consensus and Controversy." *Educational Leadership* 47: 52-54.

Slavin, Robert E. 1993. "Ability Grouping in the Middle Grades: Achievement Effects and Alternatives." *Elementary School Journal* 93(5): 535-52.

Slavin, Robert E., and Jomills H. Braddock, II. 1993. "Ability Grouping: on the Wrong Track." *College Board Review* 168(summer): 11-17.

Slavin, Robert E., and Eileen Dickle. 1981. "Effects of Cooperative Learning Teams on Student Achievement and Race Relations." *Sociology of Education* 54: 174-98.

Sleeter, Christine E., and Carl A. Grant. 1985. "Race, Class, and Gender in an Urban School." *Urban Education* 20 (April): 37-60.

Smith, Elsie J., and Lee N. June. 1982. "The Role of the Counselor in Desegregated Schools." *Journal of Black Studies* 13(December): 227-40.

Smith, G. R. 1983. "Desegregation and Assignment of Children to Classes for the Mildly Retarded and Learning Disabled." *Integrated Education* 21: 208-11.

Smith, Marzell, and Charles D. Dziuban. 1977. "The Gap between Desegregation Research and Remedy." *Integrated Education* 15(November-December): 51-55.

So, Alvin Y. 1987. "Hispanic Teachers and the Labeling of Hispanic Students." *High School Journal* 71(October/November): 5-8.

Soodak, Leslie C., and David M. Podell. 1993. "Teacher Efficacy and Student Problem as Factors in Special Education Referral." *Journal of Special Education* 27: 66-81.

Spring, Joel. 1993. *Conflict of Interests: The Politics of American Education.* 2d ed. New York: Longman Publishing Group.

Stahl, Wayne K. 1979. "The U.S. and Native American Education: A Survey of Federal Legislation." *Journal of American Indian Education.* 18(3): 28-32.

Stewart, Joseph, Jr. 1977. *Second Generation Discrimination: Unequal Educational Opportunity in Desegregated Southern Schools.* Unpublished doctoral dissertation, University of Houston.

Stokrocki, Mary. 1992. "The Transmission and Reproduction of Art Culture in One Navajo Public School System." Paper presented at the Annual Meeting of the American Educational Research Association, San Francisco, CA.

Svingen, Orlan J. 1992. "Jim Crow, Indian Style," pp. 268-77 in Roger L. Nickols (ed.), *The American Indian: Past and Present.* New York: McGraw-Hill.

Swisher, Karen. 1990. "Cooperative Learning and the Education of American Indian/Alaskan Native Students: A Review of the Literature and Suggestions for Implementation." *Journal of American Indian Education* 29(2): 36-43.

Swisher, Karen. 1994a. "Education," pp. 855-68 in Duane Champagne (ed.), *The Native North American Almanac: A Reference Work on Native North Americans in the United States and Canada.* Detroit, MI: Gale Research.

Swisher, Karen. 1994b. "American Indian Learning Styles: An Assessment of Teacher Knowledge." *Journal of Educational Issues of Language Minority Students* 13(spring): 59-77.

Swisher, Karen, and Donna Deyhle. 1989. "The Styles of Learning Are Different, but the Teaching Is Just the Same: Suggestions for Teachers of American Indian Youth." *Journal of American Indian Education* (Special Issue, August): 1-14.

Swisher, Karen, and Michelle Hoisch. 1992. "Dropping out among American Indians and Alaska Natives: A Review of Studies." *Journal of American Indian Education* 31(2): 3-23.

Swisher, Karen, Michelle Hoisch, and D. Michael Pavel. 1991. *American Indian/ Alaskan Native Dropout Study, 1991.* Washington, D.C.: National Education Association.

Thompson, Frank J. 1976. "Minority Groups in Public Bureaucracies: Are Passive and Active Representation Linked?" *Administration and Society* 8(August): 201-26.

Thompson, Frank J. 1978. "Civil Servants and the Deprived: Socio-Political and Occupational Explanations of Attitudes toward Minority Hiring." *American Journal of Political Science* 22: 325-47.

Thompson, Lawrence H. 1991. "Within-School Discrimination: Inadequate Title VI Enforcement by Education's Office for Civil Rights." Statement before the Committee on Labor and Human Resources, United States Senate.

Tippeconnic, John W., III. 1991. "The Education of American Indians: Policy, Practice and Future Direction." pp. 180-207 in D. E. Green and T. V. Tonnesen (eds.), *American Indians: Social Justice and Public Policy.* Madison, WI: University of Wisconsin System, Institute on Race and Ethnicity.

Tonemah, Stuart. 1987. "Assessing American Indian Gifted and Talented Students' Abilities." *Journal for the Education of the Gifted* 10(3): 181-94.

Tonemah, Stuart A. 1991. "Philosophical Perspectives of Gifted and Talented American Indian Education." *Journal of American Indian Education* 31(1): 3-9.

Trujillo v. Garley. 1948. (D.N.M.).

Tucker, Harvey, and Harmon Zeigler. 1980. *Professionals Versus the Public.* New York: Longman.

Tucker, James A. 1980. "Ethnic Proportions in Classes for the Learning Disabled: Issues in Nonbiased Assessment." *Journal of Special Education* 14: 93-105.

Tufte, Edward R. 1974. *Data Analysis for Politics and Policy.* Engelwood Cliffs, NJ: Prentice-Hall.

Tyack, David B. 1974. *The One Best System: A History of American Urban Education.* Cambridge, MA: Harvard University Press.

U.S. Commission on Civil Rights. 1976. *Fulfilling the Letter and Spirit of the Law: Desegregation of the Nation's Schools.* Washington, D.C.: U.S. Government Printing Office.

U.S. Commission on Civil Rights. 1977. *Statement on Metropolitan School Desegregation.* Washington, D.C.: U.S. Government Printing Office.

U.S. Commission on Civil Rights. 1979. *Desegregation of the Nation's Public School: A Status Report*. Washington, D.C.: U.S. Government Printing Office.

U.S. Department of the Interior. Bureau of Indian Affairs. 1991. *American Indians Today: Answers to Your Questions*. 3d Ed. Washington, D.C.: U.S. Department of the Interior.

U.S. Senate. Committee on Labor and Public Welfare. Special Subcommittee on Indian Education. 1969. *Indian Education: A National Tragedy, a National Challenge*. Senate Report 80, 91st Congress, 1st Session. Washington, D.C.: U.S. Government Printing Office.

Useem, E. L. 1990. "'You're Good, but You're Not Good Enough': Tracking Students out of Advanced Mathematics." *American Educator* 14(3): 24-27 & 43-48.

Wainscott, Stephen H., and J. David Woodard. 1988. "Second Thoughts on Second-Generation Discrimination: School Resegregation in Southern States." *American Politics Quarterly* 16: 171-92.

Weick, Karl. 1976. "Educational Organizations as Loosely Coupled Systems." *Administrative Science Quarterly* 21: 1-19.

Weinberg, Meyer. 1983. *The Search for Quality Integrated Education*. Westport, CT: Greenwood Press.

Weisberg, Robert. 1978. "Collective vs. Dyadic Representation in Congress." *American Political Science Review* 72: 535-47.

West, Peter. 1990. "Panel on Indian Education to Suggest 'Bill of Rights.' " *Educational Week* (August 1): 39-44.

West, Peter. 1991. "Native Americans Said to Lack Clout to Improve Their Children's Schools." *Education Week* (February 27):11.

Whiteman, Henrietta. 1984. "Educational Excellence: An Indian Perspective." *Journal of Thought* 19(3):65-73.

Williams, Junious. 1979. "In-School Alternatives to Suspensions: Why Bother?" pp. 1-22 in Antoine M. Garibaldi (ed.), *In-School Alternatives to Suspension: Conference Report*. Washington, D.C.: U.S. Government Printing Office.

Wilmer, Franke, Michael E. Melody, and Margaret Maier Murdock. 1994. "Including Native American Perspectives in the Political Science Curriculum." *PS: Political Science & Politics* 27: 269-76.

Wilson, William J. 1973. *Power, Racism, and Privilege: Race Relations in Theoretical and Sociohistorical Perspectives*. New York: Macmillan.

Wirt, Frederick M., and Michael W. Kirst. 1989. *Schools in Conflict: The Politics of Education*. 2d. ed. Berkeley, CA: McCutchan Publishing Corporation.

Wolfgang, Charles H. 1995. *Solving Discipline Problems: Methods and Models for Today's Teachers*. 3d. ed. Boston: Allyn and Bacon.

Worcester v. Georgia, 31 U.S. (6Pet.) 515 (1832).

Wright, Bobby. 1992 "American Indian and Alaska Native Higher Education: Toward a New Century of Academic Achievement and Cultural Integrity," in Patricia Cahape and Craig B. Howley (eds.), *Indian Nations at Risk: Listening to the People. Summaries of Papers Commissioned by the Indian Nations at Risk Task Force of the U.S. Department of Education.* Charleston, WV: ERIC Clearinghouse on Rural Education and Small Schools.

Wright, David E., III. 1992a. Equity In Urban Service Delivery: An Analysis Of Resource Allocation in the U.S. Public Schools. Unpublished master's thesis, Oklahoma State University.

Wright, P., and R. Santa Cruz. 1983. "Ethnic Composition of Special Education Programs in California." *Learning Disability Quarterly* 6: 387-94.

Yates, Alayne. 1987. "Current Status and Future Directions of Research on the American Indian Child." *American Journal of Psychiatry* 144(9):1135-42.

Ysseldyke, James E., and Bob Algozzine. 1983. "LD or Not LD: That's Not the Question!" *Journal of Learning Disabilities* 16: 29-31.

Ysseldyke, James E., Martha Thurlow, Janet Graden, Caren Wesson, Bob Algozzine, and Stanley Deno. 1983. "Generalizations from Five Years Research on Assessment and Decision Making." *Exceptional Education Quarterly* 4(spring): 75-93.

Ysseldyke J., S. Christenson, B. Pianta, and B. Algozzine. 1983. "An Analysis of Teachers' Reasons and Desired Outcomes for Students Referred for Psychoeducational Assessment." *Journal of Psychoeducational Assessment* 1: 73-83.

Yudof, Mark G. 1975. "Suspensions and Expulsions of Black Students from the Public Schools." *Law and Contemporary Problems* 39: 374-411.

Yudof, Mark G. 1981. "Implementing Desegregation Decrees," pp. 245-62 in Willis D. Hawley (ed.), *Effective School Desegregation: Equity, Quality, and Feasibility.* Beverly Hills, CA: Sage.

Index

Ability grouping, indicators of, 54; meta-analysis of, 37. *See also* Academic grouping; Educable mentally retarded (EMR) classes; Learning disablilities (LD) classes; Gifted classes

Academic grouping, 31, 60, 86, 130; classification problems, 38; components of, 4; as conflicts with integration, 35; controversy with, 31; current use of, 31; deleterious effects of, 40; and discrimination, 34; and educational attainment, 42; effectiveness of, 35; permanence of, 37; prevalence of, 31; and special education, 40; three broad categories of, 31; used to sort students, 4

African Americans, 97; administrators, 86; dropout rates, 43; graduation rates, 93; suspensions, 92; teachers, 86, 91-93, 100, 126

Alabama, 134, 138; case studies, 99

Alaska, 3

Allen v. Merrell (1956), 9-10

American Indian Education Program, 120-27

American Indian Education Summit, 30

American Indian education: during the Civil War, 12; political history of, 7; public schools, 9

American Indian enrollment, by school type, 16

American Indians: and academic grouping, 34, 38; administrators, 28, 52, 75, 83-84; below the poverty level, 19; counselors, 114, 125; defined, 3; denied equal educational opportunities, 130; determinants of representation, 78; determinants of representation among school administrators, 82; determinants of representation on school boards, 80; determinants of second generation discrimination factor, 96; determinants of suspensions, 93; determinants of teacher representation, 85; and dropout rates, 43; and educational attainment, 43; and educational policymaking, 21; and gifted and talented programs, 33; and income,

About the Authors

DAVID E. WRIGHT, III is Special Studies Coordinator for the Oklahoma State Department of Health.

MICHAEL W. HIRLINGER is Associate Professor of Political Science at Oklahoma State University.

ROBERT E. ENGLAND is Professor of Political Science at Oklahoma State University.

ISBN 0-89789-531-2

HARDCOVER BAR CODE